Reflections
of an Oreo Cookie

Reflections of an Oreo Cookie:

Growing up black in the 1960s

by

Gerald Thompson

Library Research Associates Inc.
Monroe, New York
1991

"Caged Bird" from *SHAKER WHY DON'T YOU SING?* by Maya Angelou. Copyright (c) 1983 by Maya Angelou. Reprinted by permission of Random House, Inc.

MUSIC IS MY MISTRESS by Edward Kennedy Ellington, 1973. Doubleday & Company. Permission is granted by Doubleday a division of Bantam, Doubleday, Dell Publishing Group, Inc.

Library Research Associates, Inc.
Dunderberg Road RD#5, Box 41
Monroe, New York 10950

Library of Congress Cataloging-in-Publication Data:

Thompson, Gerald, 1956-
Reflections of an Oreo Cookie: Growing up black in the 1960s/ by Gerald Thompson.
p. cm.

ISBN: 0912526-53-X: $24.95
I. Thompson, Gerald, 1956- . 2. Afro-American--Biography.
I. Title
E185.97 T54A3 1991
973'.04907302--dc20 90-27116
[B] CIP

Dedication:

In the house of race you know of the sun. You know of its warmth and the strength sunlight brings. In the house of race you know not of the sky. In that house you see only what man has made. Without knowledge of the sky, one will grow up to chase the sun. Chase the sun and you will forever go in circles. Find the sky and the sun will come to you.

Tommie L. Thompson
December 20, 1922 - October 6, 1989

Table of Contents

Author's note

This is a work of perceptions. It is only as real as the monsters under a child's bed. The people, incidents and opinions expressed were whispered to me by these creatures. I am told that they fear the light. Bringing these memories out of the dark I hope will allow me to sleep without a night light forevermore.

An Introduction

This book is a personal narrative of events that make up my life. It is a record of my perspective of the reality I lived. I have done everything in my power to be true and honest to the spirit of what went on in those days some refer to as the 60s. What I recall of those years differs in many respects from what I see projected on television on shows like *The Wonder Years* and *China Beach.* I may be thirty-something, but my fears and dreams differ from that show as well.

I recall a time when the word "freedom" was heard quite often. I sang the theme of *Green Acres* with more spirit and joy than any Beatle tune I knew. For me the sixties was *Raisin in the Sun, To Kill a Mockingbird, Guess Who's Coming to Dinner, Lilies of the Field* and any John Wayne movie. I believed in God, Country and Dreams Deferred. I was four when the year 1960 was half over. I was 13 when 1970 began. I recall *Amos and Andy, The Mickey Mouse Club* and *Bozo Circus* with equal pleasure. I never paid much attention to the Rolling Stones, or Vietnam. The peace movement was a far second to equal rights. Kennedy and King were equals. And my father was the greatest human on earth. This was my time of youth.

I mark the year 1965 as the end of my childhood. This work will tell you why. It is not my intention to say things that will even the score of past hurts; in fact I have chosen my words in such a way as to keep facts from obscuring and distracting from the message and essential truths I am trying to convey. For example:

I tell of a job I did not get. The odd thing was that the personnel department called me and said that based on what information they had, I could file a discrimination suit. I chose not to. Coming out of the interview I knew that if this man were black I could not work for him. I knew that if I were white I could not work for him. Qualifications be damned, there are just certain people you do not wish to work for. I don't think it is important for any one to know the name of the company, the person who interviewed me, or what was said during the interview. Those are facts that would get in the way of the message.

That was the day I placed racism over my own character flaws as to why I was unemployed. I became blind to the fact that even if nine of ten employers were not going to hire blacks, one in ten *would*. And that one person of ten would see only an immature, bitter and resentful potential worker.

I have tried, when ever possible, not to allow hindsight to play a major role in describing how I acted back then. However, with age comes understanding; children can be cruel without premeditation. In cases where hurt was caused in ignorance, I admit to softening the light to give benefit of doubt.

My intent is to promote understanding. That is why certain graphic words and descriptions are left out. Obscenity had no place in my father's house. It has only the role it rates in my story. I do not believe that four letter words equate to reality. Using them gets in the way of what causes the true damage to one's self-image.

Some facts confuse rather than enlighten. I say we had two dogs. The fact is we owned four. I saw no point in introducing each dog and its history. These two dogs are composites of the four dogs to enable the story to progress smoothly. We moved into the house in April of 1965. My mother's birthday is in April. The spirit and importance of moving in April is conveyed to you more, I feel, by making moving day and my mother's birthday the same day. That's how we felt about the move. Whatever day in April it was, that house was my mother's birthday present.

I have done everything possible to allow the bigots and haters to stay safely beneath their rocks. It is better not to hurt those whom I might paint in a manner that reflects my own prejudices and ignorance…just to get one devil. I offer insight, not lists of names.

Stories listed as being written by William Lucas were in fact written by Gerald Thompson. Those stories do not match word for word what I wrote at the time described. What remains of my writing efforts from that time, are the 17th or 95th revision of a work. I recreate them in spirit, if not in fact.

I have compressed time, places and people. This is to imitate how my memory works. While life is full of events, I remember only a few. As my father's life began to fade, my view of what was important narrowed to him. My work reflects this. Major players who were important in my life, are absent from this work, not because of lack of value, but because of lack of room.

I could have hidden behind a pen name and told this story in a manner that on the surface would appear more honest. To do so, would be equal to using my color to hide my own lack of character. What pain I may inflict on people by seeking the truth cannot be worth the price, unless I am willing to accept responsibility for what I have done. You may not agree with what I say. You do not have to believe what I say. But know one thing, I can look you in the eye and say, "This was my world."

Gerald Thompson
28 November 1990

Chapter one

Black butterfly

We sent our mother home about 6:00 p.m. and together, my brother and I waited for our father to die. Jason and I had arrived at the hospital parking lot at the same instant. I had traveled 200 miles and he 40; yet like a missile launch...our arrivals at the designated area were simultaneous. Father had called out; not with words, but with the force of his will. His last attempt to bring us back together as brothers. Together, we watched over him; together, as always, his faithful dutiful sons.

Perceptions would say this was not possible for two black men for a black father is not around; a black father is not the center of the family; a black father is not the hero. No one ever told my father, or he wasn't listening. Nothing could break him down but time just wore him out. Heart surgery, kidney failure, dialysis, kidney transplant, cancer of the pancreas...five years of fighting...used him up. The lasting image I hold is of a giant oak, knocked down in a storm; an oak that didn't know it was down, so in the spring new growth emerged. The roots were deep and solid and with its top touching dirt, the plant saw hope. In time, the tree would turn itself toward the sky, off the ground. Lots of thoughts pass through your mind at such a time.

He had not eaten a solid meal in eight months, yet his arms looked as solid as stone. I was grateful for that. In death he would still appear strong. I tried to think of good times and could find none. Much of my youth had been blacked out but in forgetting the bad, I had lost the good as well.

The bad began in 1965 when we moved into a new home; his dream house. He had bought the land in 1959, when the community of Cherokee Springs had been a town for only two years. In 1965, Cherokee Springs was well established, growing and white.

The property was on the borderline of two school districts; fate or bad luck put us in harms way. One high school, Cherokee Springs, was 50-50 white and black; the other high school was all white. Immersed in white society for five years, the blacks at the high school (Daniel Boone High) saw us as Oreo Cookies (black on the outside, white on the inside) and demanded that we choose.

My brother went black in high school (1969-1973) I tried to walk a middle ground (1970-1974). The only thing you find in the middle of the road are yellow lines and dead animals. There was no middle, not then. In many ways my spirit was broken in high school. White bigotry could not defeat me, black peer pressure did.

During the long wait, we were on opposite sides of the bed. Jason looking out the window, I sitting, pretending to read a book. Most people never understood that our love for one another never failed. Hate and love can co-exist. Hate is a temporary thing; love is like breathing, you stop breathing you die. I took breathing seriously.

When I was young I suffered from asthma. Drawing breath was not an easy or obvious a thing for me. Funny thing about life, once you start seeing things from a slightly different angle, you can't stop. I was born with a tendency to use my left hand. Years of peer pressure has caused me to use my right hand for everything but writing. If I had figured out how to write with my right hand I would have. And my eyes have been the topic of discussions for years. They were the eyes of my father's mother. None of her children or any other grandchild has her eyes. To some the color is brown. To other's they appear green; a few have called them hazel. Once a photographer called them magic. I thought the whole thing silly, all this fuss over color; I still needed glasses to see.

I remember a time when the world saw me as colored and to be called black was an insult. I was proud of being a Negro until I learned "Black was beautiful." Today the word black has too many negative overtones, so I should be referred to as an "African-American"(which sounds a lot like "Afro- American"). My solution to all this was to say I belonged to the Human Race. That I was Lucas. Nothing more needed to be said.

When I see a rainbow, I see more than the primary eight colors. The complexion of tones I see have no names, and I lack the vocabulary to describe what I witness in the sky. If a blind person were to ask you what color is the wind, would you have an answer? To the individual without sight, someone who has developed a mental image of "green grass," "blue sky," "white clouds" and "invisible wind," to that blind person...could invisible be a color like magenta or metallic?

My parents grew up during the depression in the deep south. Because of them, my value system differed from my fellow classmates. Money was less important than a good reputation, and making the right buy was more important than how much you paid for it. What is the price of a smile worth? When I came into the hospital room, my father would smile. He never spoke the word love in his life time; that smile said more.

When some one who is white calls me Nigger, I smile. I know that I am not. Yet one day a black man said I was treating him like a slave. I saw red and would have punched him had he been white. Imagine a Jew calling another Jew a Nazi. That is how I felt. The only thing that prevented me from hitting him was knowledge of his heritage, he was third generation inner city.

I am 1st generation city. Both my parents were children of farmers. My parents emigrated North after World War II. Certain words carry more meaning for me than to a third generation. I have seen my great-grand mother's identification salve bracelet. I knew what the land meant to my parents. I could look at my grandparents and know that their parents knew slavery first hand. So the word *slave* had a deeper meaning for me than it did for him.

We use the word *Black* as if it were a single thing, yet there are many shades of black. My father's grandmother was a full blooded Native American. His features reflected this with straight black hair, a skin that summer turned a reddish tone; never a heavy beard.

My mother's black reflected a slave owners way with his property. She was light skinned, small of frame, fragile in appearance; but deceptive in her strength. She was a weeping willow tree to my fathers oak. She could be bent by the storm, but never broken.

My father was born and raised in Alabama. He never finished high school and he lied about his age to join the Army (World War II) serving in the Pacific. He was tall in stature. When I was small he was a giant, as I grew he became larger than life.

My mother was from a proud Kentucky family. Being in her presence is like looking up in the sky after a terrible storm and seeing a multi-hued rainbow. Her beauty is ageless. Her worth without price. Her devotion without peer and her heart the personification of kindness.

Into this union first came a son, who died at the age of two, followed by Jason and me. Sixteen years later at the time of the greatest strain another son, a gift from God. My mother was 42. It brought another focus back into their marriage; it gave Jason and me something to agree on. Fate always stepped into our lives at the oddest moments.

As my father grew weaker, he wanted my mother's mother to live with some one else. At 97 years of age she left my father's house on my birthday, went to Charleston, South Carolina, she arrived just in time for Hurricane Hugo. After the hurricane, Granny came back to stay.

My last and most violent argument with Daddy was over Granny being told to move. He believed the strain on my mother to care for him and her mother was too much. Granny preferred our house, but he had his way. Fate brought her back. During one of his bad moments, Granny went into his room and held his hand.

This single act removed all trace of resentment in my mother's eyes. Until the end, she saw Daddy in the eyes of her youth. At 97, Granny saw things more clearly than any of us.

When we were good we were my father's sons, when we were bad, we were my mother's boys. We were dressed like twins, but were miles apart in temperament.

My brother was tall, skinny, athletic, friendly, easygoing, popular and smart. I was short, stout, uncoordinated, sickly (asthma and allergies), opinionated, and not so popular.

Before the move, we were brothers with typical sibling rivalry; nothing more or less. We lived in a neighborhood that was changing. All the whites were moving out as the blacks moved in. We shared an apartment house with relatives, my family lived downstairs, my aunt, uncle and cousins upstairs.

We were surrounded by kids our own age, all black, and I thought we were the typical American family, just like in "Leave it to Beaver," "Donna Reed" or "Father knows best." Every family I knew had a hard working respected father, a good looking mother and a well-kept home or apartment. Living nearby were grandparents and other relatives.

After the move, I kept hearing that this was not normal, that the black family was breaking down, that homes were run by fat dominating females, that fathers were never around and never worked. That drugs were easily accessible... I would go home and watch my father go to his second and sometimes third job, and wonder just what they were talking about. The only drug I knew was cigarettes. We owned a dog, walked to school, came home for lunch and felt loved, protected and safe. In a different world my father could have built his house, and in time we would have come to accept the new place as a real home...not a fortress against racism!

We always knew we were going to move. Daddy had been buying stuff for years. Our playroom had been taken over by floor tile, sinks, light fixtures, doors, windows, a washer, dryer, refrigerator and on and on...all still packed up and waiting. Daddy was over forty, married for 15 years with two growing children when he set out to make his dream real. He delivered mail for a living, but this did not prevent him from wanting more for his family.

That first summer, people mistook him for the gardener. The house was such a fine house that people could not conceive of a black family living there except as servants. People would pull up into the drive and ask how much my father charged. They would try to pump him for information about the folks who owned the place. Daddy got a kick out of letting people think he just worked there.

I have often wondered if this mistaken identity in some way saved us from violence. After months of praising Dad for his hard work, people claimed he would not keep the house up, and that property values would go down. It was not until we registered for school that the truth sunk in—the gardener owned the place. I think they were embarrassed. After registration the name calling began.

In my mind I thought of the new house, the better school…as a place like where we lived, only someplace else. I was not into deep thought back then, but was quiet and gullible. I had been told there were giant redwood trees near the school yard with a twelve story tree house. It did not occur to me that if the trees were any where near the school, I should have been able to see the tops of them from just about anywhere. The same could be said for the robot which somehow never made it to class.

Besides being a sucker for any tall tale, I was accident prone. Because of my size I was not allowed to play in the baseball games except as the designated catcher. The day I was hit in the head by a baseball bat…(broke the bat) proved what I had been hearing for years-how hard a head I had. In some ways I was real proud of my injury.

One day my head wasn't hard enough. Heading down into the basement to give Slurp (our dog) some water, I tripped on a house shoe. I fell down the entire flight of stairs landing in Slurps food dish, a fact Slurp was not happy about. Up those stairs I ran, screaming…my head bleeding. They rushed me to the hospital, the result being a tiny permanent bald spot, which unfortunately has grown through the years.

Another time, playing a game called run down, much like tag, except that bikes were used, I was dodging the bikes and I slipped on the sidewalk leaving half my kneecap behind me. It took two years to get rid of the limp.

Important events in history took second place to the happening in my household. In 1963 my father bought a 1962 Blue Thunderbird with a white vinyl top, electric windows, white wall tires with fender skirts. The ignition was on the left had side, something all left handed people can appreciate. To open the trunk you lifted the head of a bird. From a distance the sloping hood was like a four eyed hawk coming toward you. I loved that car. That year, 1963, was also the year Kennedy was shot.

JFK was important to me after he died for I saw the affect this had on my parents and on other adults. I felt a need to find out why, however, that was years in the future. At that time it was only the car. It had bucket seats, I always rode in front my mother and older brother in the back. It had a steering wheel what moved to the side when you got out. And the ride of that car. Daddy could make you think you were on air. No child ever got car sick when he drove. Slurp loved the car too. It had tiny rear windows, and he would stick his head out and smile all day long. It wasn't just a plain blue either, it was Acapulco Blue. The best blue of them all.

We lived across the street from a Catholic church, and the only time we saw large groups of white people was on Sunday or in the local stores. Whites that lived on the block were old people who kept to themselves in hostile isolation. We didn't enter their yards to retrieve our baseballs. We would lower our voices when passing by their windows.

School was mostly black faces. We didn't consider Italians white, but we thought them all mob related and wanted to be on their good side. Hispanics (or Chicano or Mexicans) were around (but you couldn't understand them) so they were pretty much ignored (at this time I had no informed views about the evils of stereotyping). Jews were white but their parents owned everything so you didn't say anything where they could overhear. This just left the Polish and Orientals for what racial slurs were slung.

(Catholics didn't attend our schools, and we all knew they kept guns buried in the basement for the day the Pope told them to take over).

For fun we played baseball in the streets with real bats, not sticks like those wimps in New York. It took skill to hit that ball between cars, houses and trees. Sports included tackle football, bicycle races and making the biggest snow ball ever. Groups of fifty to a hundred would create balls four stories high that didn't completely melt until the first week in July.

We rushed home to watch Bozo Circus at lunch time, threw rocks at passing cars and didn't have a clue what drugs were. Liquor was around our house, but such was the power of my fathers rules, it was never touched (except that one time, and the taste was so bad I never tried it again). Root beer was so much better than Miller, A & W Root Beer, in the big mugs.

The Cubs were the team to cheer, as was any show that had a black face was a show to watch (which was why we watched Lawrence Welk). It was a time of Sonic Booms (which I blamed for a window I broke) hula hoops and slinky's. We were always flattening a piece of silly putty on the Sunday comics, amazed that the picture would come off and appear on the putty.

It was a time of super balls (I could never get mine to bounce over the house), Rice Krispies, (no matter how close I put my ear to the bowl I never heard "Snap, Crackle, Pop"(for years I thought I was pouring the milk on wrong); the white knight who could turn your dirty cloths white; a giant who lived inside little bags of detergent. I would wait and wait for his fist to come up out of the washer and it never did.

It was also the time of the Civil Rights Movement, freedom rides, Jim Crow and separate but equal. When we went for a ride, it was always in our Sunday best. We weren't allowed to eat or drink anything before the trip, and it would do no good to ask to stop for the rest room. There were none to go to.

I knew I was Colored, but I wasn't sure what that meant. I did know I was William Lucas, with a Capital W and a large L. I had always been too smart for my own good. I didn't think it was necessary to learn my A B C's (after all each year in school they had them plastered all over every wall, and I could read); why waste time memorizing. It didn't occur to me that those letters could come down from the walls.

Things that occurred to me, somehow didn't seem to be the same things that occurred to other people. When I learned I had to go to nursery school, I demanded to know why Slurp didn't have to go. He was older than I was. I never got a good answer. At the pre-school I cried for Slurp. If I had cried for my mother I would have been considered normal. I was considered to be socially maladjusted because I was screaming for a dog. (I remember that day, and I remember why I was screaming for the dog instead of my mother. If I had cried for my mother it wouldn't have done any good).

There were just a few things that kept this time from being perfect. The fact that Jason and I were always dressed alike was one of them. Because we didn't grow at the same rate, I got to wear the identical clothing many years running. I couldn't wait for the day I could pick my own.

Sundays we had to eat breakfast together Daddy was working so many jobs, that the only time he had with the family was on Sunday before church. We had to say a prayer and eat anything that was on our plates. One day I sat for eight hours over cold pancakes and dried syrup, hoping they would disappear.

Church was okay, except my father wanted us to have good hair. So he simulated that fact with some yellow stuff that turned our hair straight. Think of pouring Elmer's glue on your hair, that's how I felt about this stuff. It was like concrete when it dried. After church I would rush home and try to wash it out. It never did any good, it took at least two days before water would do anything but roll off this stuff.

My mother attended a Baptist church, Daddy attended a Methodist, so my brother and I had our choice. We never missed a Sunday. Even then I was aware of the differences in the two churches. One thing about the Baptist church bothered me. You would enter the church and have to walk past the nurses' station. I associated the quality of the sermon by how many people had to be taken back to that station (all those people seized by the spirit and lead off; or those who fainted and had to be carried). When the people got to shouting and jumping I didn't know what was going on. It was in total contrast to the Methodist church.

At my father's church you knew when the sermon would end; something you could never be sure about at the Baptist church. Things were quiet and sedate (my father was a Deacon so I got to sit alone). No shouting, but most important, it was short.

Oddly enough, when the time came to choose a church I chose my mothers. It seemed to have more potential. I believed in what was said, and it was many a year before I got rid of the guilt of playing records on Sunday.

In the world before 1965, I felt safe. After 1965, my youth went away. I wrote while in high school,

Did I awake today?

by William Lucas

I just don't know what is going on any more. Is this another nightmare? Am I still asleep? Why...can't these dreams stop? I can see nothing...hear nothing...not even the sound of my own voice! MY mind seems to be stuck in a rut, like a needle on a record. I can only remember songs: "Rain drops keep falling on my head..."

Each night, I dream of "The green, green grass of home." Am I dead? Why is everything so dark? Why can't I see? "Who can make a sunrise?" Why did this happen to me. Where can I find my "Yesterday?" Please someone find my mother. Ask her to go to my bedroom and wake me up! Please? Did anyone hear...

I am so alone, "why can't my finger reach," I reach out for love and attention but my fingers don't reach... "I can't stop loving you" Ray Charles.

Why didn't the "Sunrise...Sun set?" heaven help me. "Heaven help us all." Everybody loves a nut. But why do they hate me. I never wore a white sheet, I never burned a cross. "The thrill is gone." Where was that place where "trouble falls like lemon drops?" Somewhere. If birds go there why can't I?

Have you ever seen a Black Butterfly. I saw one once, newly emerged from it's cocoon and trying to fly. Oh, my God! Did he try. He flapped those wings...so hard! So fast! I thought he would die from exhaustion, long before he ever became airborne.

This butterfly, so unlike the others. So much darker than its brothers. It seemed doomed. Doomed from birth to live a half-life unable to lift off the ground. I thought I would cry. But the butterfly did not die, did not stop trying. Then to my surprise he started to rise. First he fluttered and stumbled...and then...then he rose and lifted up in the air...in a way...in a way...that no other butterfly would even think to try.

So high! So very very high! A dark dot in the sky. But then, some kids, who happened to be walking by saw my little black butterfly. They decided to try to catch this mahogany insect. and catch him they did.

Not interested in beauty. Not caring of uniqueness. They just ripped his wings off and left. But the butterfly continued to try. Continued to flap stubs in an effort to regain the sky. But all he could do now was die.

And if he had lived, the world might be full of small yet beautiful black butterflies. I wonder if they would have stopped and caught an ordinary white butterfly. I wonder...

Am I awake?

Chapter two

Stranger in a strange land

Cancer can be a slow death. I tried to spend quality time with my father. As a maker of industrial training programs, I was expected in Mississippi for three weeks of location shooting. As a son, I felt my place was at his side. On Thursday he would have cancer surgery...if the news was good I would go. If the news was bad, I would stay. That night they took out his pancreas, gallbladder, spleen and half his stomach.

Early the next morning I went to intensive care to find out the prognosis. The doctor said he would be around for a while, but the future was in God's hands. I went in to see my father. His hair which was gray, seemed to have turned a pure white. I leaned over him:

"Daddy?"

His eyes opened instantly, and he knew who I was.

"I think, they got everything." He nodded, and tried to say something; but no sound came out. He held out his hand, I took it and he held it for a long time.

"I have to go. I'll be back in three weeks, will you be here?"

He smiled, and mouthed, "Yes."

I called my mother and told her of his condition. She said I should go. Life has to continue...I hung up and headed for Mississippi.

*****

My mothers birthday is April 1st. We moved in April 1, 1965. That first day, the police pulled up and asked what we were doing there. I said, "We live here."

They went away, but my mother was upset...her birthday ruined.

It's hard to realize that it was not so simple to own property in the United States of America, if you were not the right sort of person. Many deeds had restriction to prevent people of color from living on the premises in any capacity but servants. People would not sell to you, banks would not finance loans, outside of certain areas where you were supposed to live.

The person who sold my father the property in 1959 first transferred it into a secret land trust (which are legal in Illinois) and the land trust turned around and transferred title of the property to Daddy. At that time, the lot was in the middle of no where, surrounded by farm land, before Malls were built, and before Cherokee Springs began to expand north.

The house was built of stone, ranch style, spread over six lots, with a circle drive. The house was designed by my father with plenty of closet space, a living room, family room, two bathrooms, kitchen, a utility room (for the washer and dryer), front and rear patio, four picture windows, full basement and only two bedrooms. No guest room, no easy exit from the basement. In time (24 years) the basement became a reflection of the upstairs with paneled walls, two bathrooms, two bed rooms, a circle bar (hand built), fire place and a kitchen dining area. He tiled the entire basement floor, including the stairway (upstairs are those tiny wood squares, which today would cost more than the house did to build). And the garage was 1/2 inch short of being a two car garage.

We moved into a shell. The only completed room was the kitchen. No painting, landscaping, hung doors, window blinds, or anything else had been done (the basement was concrete and bare wood frames, where rooms would one day go). The driveway was dirt, the rear patio still a decade from completion. No trees, scrubs or even level ground. All those things in my father's mind were extras. When he borrowed $20,000.00 to build a house, that's all he built.

With all that work to do, it is easy to see now, why he was mistaken for hired help. Daddy's secret desire as a youth was to be an architect. At some point he settled for working in the post office. He had all the skills a master builder needed. He just lacked access into the craft. This house was to last 200 years.

If he had built and sold the house; then built and sold the next one...today we would be rich. He chose stone, because stone could be bought and stockpiled. He built in the middle of winter when construction work was slow.

He used retired people off his mail route (who wanted something to do) and he worked on the house himself.

The house was near his mail route. He knew the area and the people were friendly, so he assumed that they would welcome him.

At first, people drove by the house and shouted, "Nigger!" Twenty, twenty-five times a day. Each morning our front area would be littered with trash. We would just clean up and continue trying to fix things up. Since we had moved in April, we continued to go to our old school (it was only six miles away) and kept the move secret from our friends. My mother is light skinned, and the people seeing her drop us off at the house each afternoon (after school) assumed we were just visiting our father.

My mother had the habit of riding in the back of the car, which led many to feel Daddy was her chauffeur. I have wondered if this habit did not come about from the displeasure people showed when she road in front. Once my mother attended a convention. The parking attendant couldn't believe the two of them were together; he drove the Thunderbird into a wall. (Daddy never repaired the dent, because he liked telling people how it got there).

There were of course, the hate calls. These callers didn't get the reaction they were expecting.

"Hello."

"Damn niggers, get out of town."

"What? You say there are niggers in town!"

"Yes?"

"We better have a meeting about this... Honey, is my sheet ironed? Let me have your number... William get the cross ready... Where do these niggers live?... Jason, get the gasoline."

You would be surprised how many people actually thought they had gotten the wrong number. It didn't help much if they got me on the phone either.

"Hello."

"Boy, put that jungle bunny gorilla you call a father on the line."

"My name is William."

"I said put your daddy on the line, if he is your daddy?"

"Who's calling?"

"God damn it, I said put your mother fucking father on the phone."

"It's not nice to swear."

"Your mammy home."

"Didn't Al Jolson sing that?"

After awhile, they hung up. Jason and my mother would just drop the phone in its cradle without saying a word. Sometimes the callers would try trickery to get past me.

"Let me speak to your father."

"Who's calling please."

"His mother."

I hung up the phone, and for the first time I was upset.

"Who was that?" Daddy asked.

"She said she was your mother."

"My mother's dead."

"I know."

Because of people throwing things out their windows and the yelling Jason and I began to play more and more toward the rear of the house. A huge mound of dirt left over from when they dug the basement became the mountain. And triumph was walking across one end of the mountain to the other. Sometimes we even got Slurp up there with us.

Slurp was a tiny dog, part Chihuahua and part something else. He was large for a chihuahua, but small enough for some people to refer to him as a giant rat. He was multi-colored, black, brown, and white, and his ears bent over except when he heard a sound then they would shoot straight up. Slurp knew every inch of our property line, and anything that came within centimeters of touching the DMZ, Slurp would let the world know.

Slurp could jump ten feet straight up in the air. And many a six- footer ran screaming when this tiny mutt would throw its entire body upward toward a throat. People never took the time to find out was Slurp was all intimidation. He never bit anyone in his life. If you stood your ground Slurp would always grab a piece of clothing and never skin. He had only been in one real fight in his life, and that was against a collie. The collie sat on Slurp and that ended the fight.

One night our windows were shot out. It took two hours for the police to come; Slurp went crazy. We had to lock him in the bathroom. Slurp was smart enough to know how doors worked. Not smart enough to know that they only swung one way. He had a habit of leaping against doors to open them. This was 2:00 A.M., the bathroom was amplifying Slurps barks, and every ten seconds he would leap against the door. Boom! Boom! Boom!

The police who didn't quite know what to expect, were a little unnerved by this barking and banging against the door. During the 45 minutes they were there, they kept looking toward the bathroom. Slurp kept hitting that door. Boom! Boom! Boom!

After looking at our windows they concluded that it was the work of a BB gun. Most likely a kid on a dare. My father didn't believe them. As the tension mounted, one of the police officers asked what kind of dog we owned.

"A Chihuahua," my father said. The cops didn't believe him. The last words as they left the house, were for us to keep the dog on a leash.

The phone calls turned real after that. We were no longer allowed to answer the phone. My mother would just disconnect the phone until Daddy came home. Then fate stepped in. Martin Luther King came to Chicago, August 1965. With King only 35 miles away and looking for a confrontation, things swiftly turned around. We were never official members of the movement. What we did we did on our own. Daddy never wanted us to be used as pawns. Perhaps he used the threat of Dr. King as a way to protect us.

A man also died at that time. A local hood, they said. His body jumped in the field behind our house. Some have said this was the man who shot at our windows.

Dad kept saying, "We are not here to integrate. We are here to live. We just want to be left alone."

He never called for help.

The house faced farm land to the west (mostly soy beans) and farm land on either side and behind (corn). The land to the west was owned by Dutch farmers named Brown. The Browns cared only about farming and hated being bothered. When a committee came to have them sign a petition against us the Browns said, "They don't bother me. I like that. You come on my property again, I shoot you. Get out."

Not modern farmers, Mr. Brown would pull weeds by hand. They (his only son Mack) would be out in the fields as long as the sun was up. Because they just wanted to be left alone they became the only friendly faces for a long time.

We would wave at one another every day. I don't think we exchanged ten words that year, but a thousand and one waves did pass between us. We did our best never to cross their land. When we explored, it was on the land behind the house.

As time went along we became the only people Mr. Brown would talk to. He would walk up and down his fields pulling weeds by hand. He would lie down on the ground to see if anything new had shown up. Once he was on the ground, a passing car stopped. The driver assumed he must have had a heart attack. Mt. Brown threatened to sue the man for every soy-bean that got trampled by his rescuer. My brother and I became two of the few allowed to step on his prized soil.

Mack Brown would one day buy an enclosed tractor with AM and FM radio, air conditioning and plush seats. The same year Mr. Brown complained about a Cadillac dealer who would not sell him a Caddy without air. (They had to special-order a Lincoln to get what they wanted). Like us they just wanted to be left alone in their own world.

Cherokee Springs did many things to make life less than easy for us. We were the only school-age children in a two mile radius. Our house was located in such a way that all the school buses that serviced Cherokee Springs had to pass by our door. However, the school board insisted that my brother and I walk one mile north (no sidewalks then or now) on the highway, board the bus at the cross street, then ride the bus headed south (pass our door) into town and school.

Daddy thought this was stupid and dangerous, and would not let us walk. During the first week of school for the next five years, no bus would stop. We would call the school and they would say we could not expect special treatment and other children had to walk to a bus stop. Of course, they had side walks and other children were being picked up. Only the fact that the bus company was on my father's mail route allowed a compromise to take place. The bus company on its own, would stop at the house to pick us up after about a week had gone by. Each spring until we left Cherokee Springs schools to go to high school, no bus would stop at first. We would wait and watch the buses pass by until finally my mother would have to drive us to school.

In some ways it was bad once we got on the bus. Cherokee Springs had three school buildings, but the same buses serviced each building. The Jr. High at 8:00, 4th thru 6th at 8:30 and Pre-School to 4th at 9:00; which meant I would get on the bus at 7:05 (first stop from the bus garage) and get off at 8:50 (after picking up and delivering the other schools) to travel 4 miles. With variations, this held true for five years. The trip home was the same. I so much wanted to walk, but this was not allowed.

When we moved our bikes were taken away. We were never allowed to own one again. Mass transit had not made its way to the area. Once in a great while I would walk the four miles into town. This had a measure of danger to it some people thought it was funny to swerve in your direction.

Before the move Jason and I got along, until we got on each others nerves. We would play two man baseball, play catch, work in the yard. I began to read, write stories and watch TV., Jason started to play sports, listen to the radio and ignore me. Even the long bus rides started to reflect differences in our attitudes. Although I considered the back of the bus the best place in all the world to ride (there you could be bounced in the air over bumps, and had an unrestricted view), I was a liberated Negro, who did not sit in the back of the bus. I sat in the front seat just behind the driver. Jason sat somewhere in the middle on the opposite side.

I would wait until the bus was in sight before I ventured out the door. Jason was outside waiting twenty minutes before the bus was due. Those bus rides got to be boring very quickly. None of the kids would talk to us, and many avoided sitting next to us until all the seats were taken. I began to pass the time by making up games to amuse myself. I would read aloud license plate numbers of cars (only I read them backwards, on seeing 122024 I would yell 420221). I started telling jokes and making up tall tales. My first really successful story was Grapie the Great Grape.

Grapie the Great Grape

Once upon a time in the great city of Grapeville, there lived a grape. Not an ordinary grape; but Grapie the Great Grape, the greatest grape in all the great history of the great city of Grapeville. Why, even Grapie the Great Grape's family was great. He was related to Alexander the Grape. And when he was little he was so great, that one day he was stepped on. And he didn't give a wine. That was Grapie the Great Grape.

One day Grapie the Great Grape decided to challenge the Great Sun to the greatest stare down that ever would be, or ever was. The Great Sun accepted. So Grapie the Great Grape stared at the Great Sun. And the Great Sun, stared at Grapie the Great Grape. Hour after hour, after hour, after hour they stared.

Until Grapie the Great Grape started to lose, he got smaller, and smaller. Wrinkle-lee-er and wrinkle-lee-er. He turned in RA SON the Great Raisin.

And do you know the moral of this story?

Never challenge any one: Bigger, Better, Stronger, or Smarter than you. Or you will lose.

This story and about 75 others was submitted to my high school magazine for writers. They were all rejected. I was telling Grapie to someone when a girl looked up, "You're that William Lucas!"

"What do you mean, that William Lucas?" I said.

"Well, when we were picking stories for the magazine, that Grape one was selected."

"Then why isn't it in the magazine?"

"When the stories are reviewed, it is without the author's name on it. When the names are later matched with the story, yours got dropped. What did you do to make them so mad at you?"

After that I only submitted one story a year to the magazine; and each year my story appeared. One time I tried to convince people that when you watched a football game, the players really were little people, no bigger than fleas. I got one girl so mad that she threatened to get Dick Buckus to prove that they were big people. Dick Buckus was on my fathers mail route, so it was no threat to me. One year he gave us a case of his "Super Crunch" candy bar, which were the worst candy I ever ate, even Slurp refused to eat them. We were always having people drop by looking for some Chicago Bear player. Only a black athlete could own such a house.

That first year I heard many jokes:

"Name three things you can't give a nigger?" (One and two are a fat lip and a job).

A bus load of niggers drove off a cliff, landed near a construction site. One of the construction workers saw the accident. He got a bulldozer, dug a huge pit and pushed the bus into it. Just as he was leveling things out, the police pulled up.

"Didn't any survive?"

"Well, a couple of them said they did. But you know how niggers lie."

Daddy had forbid us from fighting, since this would reflect poorly on all black children. In some ways he must have thought we wouldn't take him seriously since he was always disappointed that we didn't show more spunk.

One day a kid came up to me and yelled, "You niggers are ruining the world." And he hit me. I pretended nothing had happened. He hit me again. I acted like the mosquitoes were out in force. He kicked me. I asked him if he was trying to get my attention. At which point he became slightly confused. Figured I must really be tough, and perhaps I wasn't the person to cross. I do not know what caused this outburst. I was however unable to raise my right arm for the rest of the day.

Sometimes I wasn't so lucky. Pro wrestling was big in those days. And of course, we had our fanatic wrestlers. Joe, announced that he could out wrestle anyone in the school. He said he could break any hold anyone cared to try on him. When my turn came, as luck would have it a teacher walked by and assumed I was beating up on Joe. "Get your paws off him," he shouted. Joe became mute as to what we were doing, everyone else had disappeared, and I got sent to the principle's office for fighting.

One day one of our teachers showed up wearing sun glasses to class. She did not take them off and by lunch time this was a major topic of discussion. In a poor attempt at humor, I mentioned the latest issue of TV Guide that featured pictures of animal stars with sun glasses: "There was Lassie, Mr. Ed, Arnold the Pig...Miss Swain."

Well, after lunch my good buddy Joe, stood up and said, "Miss Swain. At lunch William said you reminded him of a pig with those glasses on."

I was sent to the Principle's office for having a foul mouth.

Back then, students went to the bathroom at the same time, at regular periods of the day. A monitor was selected to keep track of the boys and to report any bad behavior to the teacher. On the day Joe became monitor he reported me for intentionally missing the urinal. (Untrue, because I hadn't used the facilities that day, but you don't pass up a free trip out of class). That time I only received a verbal talking to.

Joe did not like me one bit. For show and tell he brought two African figurines from home, the kind that show natives with saucers in the lips, sticks in the nose. He drew comparisons between them and my parents, to much laughter I might add.

To be fair, there were many cases of unnecessary cruelty at this time. One girl named Jane, was sickly and missed a great deal of school. On the days she was in class and happened to come into physical contact with someone, that person was said to have *cooties*, and anyone with had to get rid of them.

The lack of knowledge about anyone's heritage was shameful. And the only true regret from those days I have, is one I committed against Herbert and his bar mitzvah. We had known each other for about four years. He had taught me how to play Simon Says in Hebrew. I was invited to his bar mitzvah. I thought of it as just a fancy birthday party, not the passage into manhood. I did not go, because I thought surrounded by all those whites, I was being set up to be made fun of. Not many people went in fact. Within a year, his family would move, so that Herbert could be around more of his kind.

Not all my trials were racially motivated either. Not being good at sports, I have had run-ins with people who are. Jason was good at sports and some of what I thought were flaws in his character, I noted in other gifted athletes. When the U.S. Olympic basketball team lost and then refused to accept the Silver metal; I was reminded of games I had played. Games I should have lost but won. The reaction was the same.

One kid, named Tom, felt his only mission in life was to beat all the sports records that his older brother had set. So obsessed with winning was Tom, that it wasn't enough to beat anyone, he had to humiliate them as well.

The two of us were paired off in a foot race. We were to run eight times around the track. Tom, decided that he was going to lap me (twice). I was slow, but not that slow, Tom collapsed about thirty feet from the finish line. I, of course, bragged about how he had lost to me.

Tom felt I had misled him about how fast I could run (my view was I was never going to beat anyone good, so why kill myself). During a baseball game, I was the pitcher. I had loaded the bases, top of the first no outs. Tom comes up to bat. He does a Babe Ruth on me (pointing out where he was going to hit his homer), I threw the pitch, he hit the ball, hard! I never saw it. He hit the ball right back to the mound. In an effort to protect my lower regions, I caught the ball.

By the second inning, I was playing first base and had committed three errors. When Tom came up to bat. He switched over to the left side of the plate (to be better able to hit the ball my way). As luck would have it, I was not even looking toward home when the ball was pitched. I only knew I was in trouble when I heard the ball strike the bat. I only pretended to do something, I lifted my glove straight up in the air (like you do when you want to answer a question in class). The ball hit the top of my glove, and stayed (it looked like an ice cream cone). Tom stormed first base intent on killing me and had to be restrained.

Jason was much the same way, his view of games was either to handicap himself (to keep it close) or demolish me. He never thought it possible that on one of his off days, I could have a great day and beat him. Any time I won, the reason had to be something else.

*****

The entire time I was in Mississippi I felt I was in hell. It reminded me of high school. Nothing went right. I would call the hospital two and three times a day for updates. I began to experience sympathetic pains. I found that on my bad nights, Daddy had a bad night. By the time I left the south, I could hardly walk and felt sick all the time.

Late one night, I awoke but I could not open my eyes. My head had detached itself from my body. I was floating over the bed. I was not breathing, my heart was slowing down. I started to concentrate. I told myself to breath, I forced my heart to beat again. Then the phone rang. It was Jason.

"They had to take Daddy back into surgery. He's bleeding inside."

I went back to Chicago. I arrived on Father's Day.

Chapter three

The wonder years

From that day on, I made special unexpected visits to the hospital. Daddy was not a reader of books, nor did he care much for TV or the radio. We did a lot of sharing space together; it seemed to be enough. Daddy once said there was no such thing as conversation without conflict. I don't know who told him that, but from the day he first said it, we had constant arguments. I miss those arguments.

*****

Seven communities fed into Daniel Boone High School which gave it a 50-50 mix. First day of high school, I wore a tie, jacket and carryed a briefcase for my father thought of high school in much the same way we used to think of college. I was approached by a black student, the first black face not related to me I had seen in five years.

"Just who the hell do you think you are?" he asked.

"William Lucas," I said.

"You ain't shit," he said then slapped me across the face. "Oreo," was his last comment.

This was 1970, a year of no middle ground. You allied yourself Black, or White but I was not aware of any of this. I had not been warned by Jason. That first day was also traumatic for my friend Rob who was jumped by a roving band of blacks to show the incoming white freshmen, who was in charge.

Rob was standing outside the nurses station with a bandaged head and a cut lip.

"What happened?" I asked.

"I don't really know. I was trying to get into my locker when I was beat up."

As we were talking a white teacher came by who instantly assumed that I was one of the blacks who hit Rob and had come back to finish the job. This teacher grabbed me and pushed me against the wall, but Rob stepped in.

"What do you think you're doing? That's my friend! Let him go."

Here was Rob rescuing me from a white teacher, who thought he was rescuing Rob from a black student.

If Rob had not been attacked, if I had not been slapped, if I had not been attacked by a teacher, then perhaps I might have chosen sides. I did not see color as a determining factor of who or who was not my friend. I did not *choose* the middle ground, it was the only place to make my stand. I was tired of being pushed around. I would decide who my friends would be, not anyone else. Me!

I hit many bottoms in high school. I got tired of "White Bashing" in the school's paper. Each week presented a *Hate Honkey, White Devil* diatribe. I kept wondering, where was the balance? I wrote to the editor to complain and the letter became a column with a byline.

Racism is jelly beans

by William Lucas

When someone offers you some jelly beans, do you stop and ask, "That depends. What color have you got?"

Yet this is exactly what we do with people. With jelly beans, we are more concerned with taste than its outer shell. With people we seem more concerned with the skin than the person inside.

Each week in this paper, in the "Soul Mouth" column, we hear how bad the white man is. We hear about conspiracies to keep the black man down. We hear about blue eyed devils out to oppress. We never hear anything about people. We never hear anything positive. Isn't this nothing more than reverse racism?

If you've never eaten a jelly bean, but someone tells you that all the orange ones are bad, you therefore go through life not eating orange jelly beans. You tell all your friends not to eat orange jelly beans because orange jelly beans are bad. Then one day, all the orange jelly beans are taken off the market, because no one is eating them. One color of the rainbow gone. The world has less variety. It doesn't matter that all jelly beans taste the same. Orange ones are bad, and its good that they are gone.

Say, I heard a rumor the other day. All green jelly beans are bad.

When this little tale appeared I was met in the locker room by twelve football sized brothers, ready to beat my face in.

"Man, you don't know what it means to be black," one said.

"Yeah, you moved from the hood," another said.

"You're not one with the movement, man."

"And you know what happens to those not in the flow."

I knew alright. So I lied. The big lie.

"Hey, I didn't write that article. It just had my name on it. Those white editors on the paper did it.

They believed me. I was safe for another day.

The reverse of this is the "all's fair in love and war" syndrome. When time came for the Senior Prom I asked this beautiful girl to go and she accepted. The problem was that the person she had rejected would not take no for an answer. He went to her and said, "William only dates white girls so he won't take you to the prom. It's a practical joke. You just wait. One of his white bitches put him up to it."

It was a big lie and she believed it. This black girl was told by a black male that I, a black man, would prefer the company of whites to such a degree that I would embarrass her to make a point.

This is the power of racism.

Racism has never prevented me from doing what I really wanted to do, but racism has caused me to impose a ceiling on what I would try.

People in pain do not always pick a correct solution. They just want the pain to stop. Think of racism as fire, and this fire must be passed through to do what you wish. Faced with pain, what becomes important enough to risk burns, and what can be passed over?

Self-imposed limitation (pain threshold) becomes a factor in whether or not to continue, or to walk away. Everyone has natural obstacles to over come. Perceptions of the unnatural can be a deciding element.

The first thing destroyed by walks through the fire is trust. At one time I had an interest in gymnastics. It was hard work and I had to overcome fear of failure and injury. I had to convince my mother to take me to practice , as she did not like to drive into Cherokee Springs. She still talks of the time she went shopping and a little baby saw her and said, "Nigger." The mother just laughed. The baby repeated the word, "Nigger" and the mother laughed harder.

A new fear was added.

"Say, William, you finally found something you're good at. But then apes are good at that sort of thing."

From that moment on I could not get past the image of people seeing me as a chimpanzee doing tricks. At some point I would have moved on to something else anyway, but I am 99% positive it would not have been that soon. One more practice could have been the difference between making a good decision or a poor one.

My girl friend had been ready to dump me over a lie by a black person who had used racial fear to get what he wanted. It was three months before she told me why she had almost not gone to the prom with me. In a way, it would have been better if I had never known. I thought of the other suitor as a friend, he thought of me as a competitor. I won the battle, we lost the war.

Anyone involved in sports knows about intimidation, the effort to gain an edge. Most young kids do not use race as a tactic unless a character-building adult shows them the advantages of it. Those on the receiving end will live through it. Those with other avenues of interest will take them. Jason played basketball in the 7th grade, but chose not to in the 8th. "It wasn't fun," was all he had to say about it. Daddy used to say, "You don't always light a fire with just one match."

There are those who never realize the difference between natural and un-natural obstacles. They do not give the benefit of a doubt to the fresh face they see. Those people are bigots until proven otherwise. You save yourself grief with pre-emptive strikes.

*****

During my second year in high school a new brother came into our lives. My parents had a hard time believing that a baby was on the way. Daddy most of all. He did not buy a single baby item until Jeffrey was delivered. That night when it became official, he emptied a store of supplies. Around the baby he seemed tentative, a fear that you can love a baby and still he might not stay.

Jeffrey became a new center of our attention. One of the first things he learned was how to imitate our father's snoring. Jeffrey would lie in the crib, pretend to snore, laugh and snore again.

At some point Jason began to get sick. He had always been thin, and never was a big eater. His grades stayed at straight A's, except for a C in gym. He got thinner and seemed to be fading away.

Daddy was working, Honey (our mother) was with the baby. I was sleeping in the same room with Jason, but that was it. One day Jason did not go to school. I came home from school and Jason was in the hospital.

On that day, Daddy wanted Slurp shot. Daddy wanted something to blame. I convinced him that if Slurp was the source, then I should be the one in the hospital.

Daddy could not understand how he could have missed Jason's illness. Our mother aged and looked like someone who had done something wrong, but is not sure what. I felt Jason had a mouth, why didn't he use it? Three days of care and Jason was back on his feet. Everything returned to normal.

*****

I am not sure when it dawned on me, but I became aware that Jeffrey, at 16, did not fully understand the situation. At 16, Jeffrey could not remember when Daddy had not been ill, so this was just another trip to the hospital, another operation.

With the birth of Jeffrey, Daddy realized that another bedroom was needed. So he built one in the basement. As I headed downstairs, I noticed a brochure on the circle bar. It was about a jazz music camp but the application had been filled out but not sent in. I wondered why, then I saw the date. It was when Daddy went in for surgery. Everyone must make choices. I told Jeffrey, "He doesn't look like he's dying. It's not like turning off a light bulb. He'll just get weaker and weaker."

"How long?"

"A month, six?"

"What's going to happen to Ma, me, the house?"

"The house is paid for. Honey will have social security and Daddy's pension."

"What good are they?"

"Don't you know what a pension is?"

"Not really."

I mumbled about what they teach in school then explained about pensions, life insurance and social security.

"So you see, there will be money. You will still have Jason. You will still have me. We will only be a phone call away."

"I feel...so selfish."

"Nothing wrong with that, we will get through this."

"You sure he's dying?"

I nodded and headed for the other bedroom that was to have been a guest room, but with my many visits was thought of as my room, the last part of the basement to be finished.

I stared at the walls until I noticed something. Then I began to check each room of the basement. Evidence of my father's illness was there in the quality of work. At the stairs that he had tiled, the work was up to his high standards.

As I moved toward the back bedroom, there was a slow decline, until the bedroom itself, complete except for the light which dangled from the ceiling. He never put the fixture into place. He never would enter the basement again.

Regardless of what I had just told Jeffrey, until I saw this, I knew he would never have done such work if he believed he could return home.

*****

It began with what we thought was another bout with his bad back which had been injured during World War II. From 1945 on, he had periods of severe pain, and needed bed rest. Because back problems are not obvious, the Post Office thought he was faking. We knew he only stopped working when the pain became too much, we knew that he went to work when the pain became bearable. As a family we resented the implied laziness of remarks about his back. John F. Kennedy had a bad back. No one called him lazy.

Daddy went to a back specialist who took x-rays, then told him to lose weight and get rest. He lost weight and the pain moved.

While he was in bed, I put together a video of his family's photos and set it to the music *In the Upper Room*. He would play it over and over. It was the first time I had a good look at his mother and father.

*****

I make my living doing industrial level training programs and documentation. When I went for my Master's Degree, I hoped one day to create my own Sesame Street, but things did not work out that way. While earning my degree, I was laid off from work and spent six months unemployed, then finally got a job with a wholesale distributor.

I work now out of a small town called Miami on the Mississippi River in the state of Iowa. Fate provided the job.

I had been working for the distributor for almost three years, but had given up hope of ever getting a job in television. I thought the time had come to be realistic, to turn my life around and make lemonade. I rose that morning intent on getting rid of all my negative attitudes. I drove onto the Expressway, turned on WGN radio, listened to Wally Phillips and thought happy thoughts.

The car in front of me, missed it's exit. The driver tried turning too late, then turned back and stalled the car. I could see I had enough room to stop, so I wasn't worried, but eased on the brake. I looked into my rear-view mirror and there was a semi-truck growing bigger and bigger. I knew he would not be able to stop.

It seemed like forever before he hit me, then pushed my Bronco into the other car for a second impact. I may have struck my head against the steering wheel and blacked out.

No damage was done to the truck and little to the car in front. My vehicle had damage to the front and rear bumpers.

When I finally got to work, I was not met with sympathy and there was no offer to send me home. I made mistake, after mistake. I was confused, I wished I had gone home, but I needed the money. By the time I went home all thoughts of staying on this job were gone.

The next day there was an argument with a fellow worker.

"Why don't you sue."

"Over what?"

"Your back. You say it's hurting you. You can make a fortune with a back injury."

"My father has a bad back. No thank you."

"Don't be stupid."

"When I knew that semi was going to hit me, I asked God to let me just walk away. that's all I wanted. I want my health, not money. Besides, insurance is paying all my bills."

"You could get more."

"A billion dollars would not be worth it to me. Not for a life in pain."

"Fool."

*****

Long walks seemed to help my back. I was walking by an office building when I decided to get a drink of water. Inside, I noticed the bulletin board and a listing struck my eye; "Wanted: entry level, television production. Miami, Iowa. Contact…"

I went in for my interview on Good Friday and the radio was playing, *We are the World.*

Chapter four

The Maleman

Daddy wanted me to tell his story. "Call it the Maleman."

"No one will buy it."

"Send it to Bill Cosby."

"I can't write the way you would like it done."

"You always do things your own way."

"It's the only way I know."

"You never did let me give you anything."

"You never offered anything I wanted."

"I can't give what I don't have."

"I can't return what I never received."

"You're a hard man."

"So are you."

*****

I called him Daddy, because he wanted it that way. I call my mother Honey, because her brother paid me five bucks to stop calling her by her first name.

When Daddy left the hospital in early July, he asked for a leather recliner. Jeffrey and I went out and bought two.

He came home on a day the temperature was 95 degrees. The house had never been air conditioned, so I went out and bought a window air conditioner which Daddy thought was a waste of money all things considered but I installed it.

He and my mother had married over the objections of both families.

"He will never be able to support you."

"She's a girl and will always be one. Marry a woman."

I think he felt his illness lent some truth to his not being able to support Honey. Some things you never out grow out. We fought our final fight over his treatment of Granny.

"To you she's an in-law, to me she's my Grandmother. Don't ask Honey to decide between you and her mother."

"Granny's been in my house for ten years. I've footed her bills, I've fed her sons. None of them have made any offer to help. Why must I always do everything? Why is everyone blaming me?"

"You've been better than them all this time. Don't stop now."

"I'm not."

"I won't let you go on hurting Honey."

"What about me? I'm sick."

"Not in the head you're not."

"You got that right."

"Granny is where she wants to be."

"When I come home, I want her gone."

*****

At 97, Granny flew to South Carolina. She never expected to see any of us again. Fate stepped in. Hugo struck the area. she was moved to a shelter. Daddy said, "If she wants, she can come back."

She did.

*****

I do not believe in conspiracies. I do believe there are independent groups of hateful people, who try to impose their views of what should be. Daddy believed in conspiracies.

There was this black surgeon who was what you think all doctors should be. He spoke to his patients in English. He did not believe in unnecessary operations, and he was a man who gave of himself gladly. He did not charge his full fee to those who could not pay it. Often he would tell them a lower charge, and then accept an even smaller figure. The official paper work would reflect full payment of the standard compensation for a procedure.

Someone added up the number of operations he did, and what they were worth and turned this doctor in to the IRS for tax fraud. By the letter of the law he was guilty. Under the law he was sent to jail. With in one year, he was dead.

It was rare to have a negro surgeon in those days. He was a hero in the community. He could have been given probation and allowed time to make full restitution. Someone chose to make an example of him.

There was another black family that moved into the area about ten miles north of us. Someone decided to put a scare into them. A explosive device was set which blew the roof off the house. The townspeople were shocked. The townspeople tried to make amends, offered to rebuild. Too little, too late.

Many in the Black community feel there are two kinds of news. If a twelve year old white boy picks up a newspaper that contains a bomb and it explodes and takes part of his hand with it, that would be front page news. There would be questions about why, and how could this happen to a boy assumed to be without guilt.

When my twelve year old cousin picked up such a paper there were comments like, "It must be gang related." and there was no outrage that such a thing could have happened. It did not make the evening news. It made page ten. Pain is the same for everyone but outrage appears to be in the eye of the beholder.

Someone is killed at a school full of white children. Counselors are sent in the next day. Someone is killed at a school full of black children and the next day is like the day before.

When reports first came out that Dr. King enjoyed the company of women, people said, "What a hypocrite, a Reverend!"

Many blacks said, "John F. Kennedy did the same thing. He was President. He was a Catholic. Who's a bigger hypocrite?"

Rumors flew that Dr. King had a church blown up and children killed, so that the Civil Rights legislation would be passed. These rumors were never exposed as lies. His failings as a human were not put in the same content of other leaders.

*****

There was an explosion at a chemical plant. Debris from the explosion flew up and came down on the roof of a cafeteria. Two people eating were killed, one of them was my Uncle. As the body was brought out, a TV news crew was on hand and taped it.

Responsible journalists that they were, they tried to contact the family. Someone did call my Grandmother, who at 87 was not certain what to believe when a total stranger called to say her son was dead. She was still standing at the phone when the pictures aired over the television. My Grandfather was watching at the time. He saw his son's body and suffered a stroke on the spot. In six months he was dead.

My father once applied for the position of Postmaster at the Falcon Heights Post Office and his application got lost in the mail.

*****

That first year, when the dead body was found behind our house, the press came. They knocked on the door and Daddy answered.

"Is the owner in?" asked the reporter.

"Yes."

"Could I speak to him please?"

"You are."

"This is your house?"

"Yes."

"This is a nice house. May I come in?"

"No."

"You don't understand. I'm from the Times. I've been in Lou Brocks house. I've been in Bob Gibson's and Jackie Robinson's."

"Well, that's nice. Goodbye."

*****

Daddy's view of the world was simple. Houses were to live in, they were not investments. The American Dream was possible.

"Long after I'm gone this house will be here."

He built too well. Buying land no one wants, you get property cheap. Spend a decade buying items on sale, when they are discontinued and you will have a lot of fine stuff (cheap). Leave unfinished anything that doesn't have to be done and you save more.

Daddy built his dream for $20,000. When it was appraised the price was $80,000. Daddy, who had worked two and three jobs to build, had to work two and three jobs (plus work on the house) to pay the taxes.

*****

Taxes have played an important role in the history of the Lucas family. It is said that after the dispute between the states, a slave owner went to his former slave and made a deal. To prevent the plantation from being broken up and sold for taxes, the former master would deed over the property to the former slave. When things returned to normal, the ex-property owner was to return the land to its rightful owner. For this my great- grandfather received 200 acres free and clear.

If you wonder why he did not try and keep the land, just remember the lyrics to the Billie Holiday song *Strange Fruit.*"

*****

People would look at the house and think we had money. In 1965, Daddy was driving a '57 Ford on the mail route. The family car was the '62 thunderbird. We watched TV on a 1949 Zenith (a wedding present) and listened to the radio on a 1950 Hi Fi System (also Zenith, a wedding present). We watched that TV until 1967 when it became impossible to find replacement tubes. The Hi Fi still in the living room, stopped working in '75. I wrecked the T.Bird in 1974. The '57 Ford was replaced in '68.

Our clothing was cleaned, washed and pressed the day after we wore them, and although recycled, always appeared new. People will assume a great deal. Dress pants are cheaper than blue jeans, which is why it was not until college that I owned a pair.

We bought winter cloths in summer, summer cloths in winter. These things were kept in closets until needed (that, after all, is what closets are for).

Daddy gave my brother and me each a baseball glove in 1963. In 1975 I took my brothers glove to college with me. I would have taken mine, but I was embarrassed by the repairs I had made over the years. In 1967 we bought the best saxophone we could find, a Selmer Mark VI. In 1990, I sold that sax for a huge profit in order to make a down payment on a house.

We were not rich, we just did the best we could. When you know what you want, then you know it can wait. And if it can wait, then you can get the best. And if you can get the best it will last. So simple.

When the store where my father worked was going to throw some Honeysuckle bushes into the trash, my father bought them for 25 cents a piece. That is why the entire back length of the house is a line of Honeysuckles. The only problem is, that it was the wrong time of year to plant and these plants were in poor shape. In twenty-nine years those Honeysuckles have neither died nor grown well. Ugly weeds. More like ugly *large* weeds.

Making a deal was the backbone of my fathers existence and it was a deal that got him the job as rural route carrier. In the 1950's there were no black rural route carriers in the state of Illinois. Some said it was because Blacks were too stupid to be able to drive a car and put mail into boxes while still in the car (on foot yes, from a car, no). My father said it was because a rural route carrier was the third highest paying job in the post office.

His chance came when he was helping with the loading of a rail car. Money was shipped through the mail and somehow, two million dollars was loaded on the wrong car and sent to South Dakota instead of San Francisco. This being Chicago, my father made a deal:

"I just told them the man said car 42, and I loaded car 24."

He got the next rural route carrier position to open up in 1956. His fellow postal workers walked off the job in protest. The effects of that year left a mark. He proved over and over he could do that job. Until the day his kidney's failed, he kept showing up for work.

One rainy day, as he was pulling away from a stop, a lady rushed out of her house waving a letter. She slipped and fell in front of Daddy's car, breaking her leg. A federal employee on official government business, cannot be stopped or held for questioning. With state, county and three different local squad cars trailing behind, he continued on his route. Nothing stops the mail from going through.

My father stood over six feet. He lacked a high school diploma. There is no telling how far he could have gone.

*****

Mail boxes are on the passenger side of the car, so Daddy had a sliding metal seat to move to the window. He would drive from the middle of the car, one hand on the wheel, and using his left foot for breaking and gas. That metal seat saved his life.

He was putting mail into a box when another car rear-ended him. The driver was uninsured and Daddy's insurance company refused to cover it because he was working at the time. The federal government only paid for time off work, claiming that because one tire was on the pavement and not off the road, he had not done enough to avoid the accident. The car was totaled, but that metal seat prevented his back from being broken. When I first started to drive, it was with the understanding that the metal seat must be in place.

Daddy got a patent on a changeable rubber stamp which he thought would be his way to fame and fortune. The post office however, wasn't interested. Just before the patent expired, Daddy heard his stamp was being used in Japan.

Daddy would pick numbers for the lottery and not have a single number show up. He bought five dollars worth of tickets every week, even in the hospital. In all his years of playing, he never won a dollar.

One time he was going to start his own business. He bought a gas station near the post office, hoping to get the contract on all the postal vehicles, or at the very least the rural route carriers. The city condemned the property to make way for an Old

Folks Home. He recovered enough to pay off the mortgage, but lost money on the tow truck, fuel and miscellaneous items such as spare auto parts and tools.

*****

My only indication of how great a strain getting the rural carrier job had been, was in realizing that 1956 was the year I was born, two months premature.

Before 1965, Daddy used to spank us with a belt that had a silver dollar as a buckle. After 1965, he never raised his, voice or his hand, to my brother or me. I think this was because he could no longer trust control of his anger if it was released. Once, Slurp jumped into the Thunderbird after Daddy had just cleaned it. Daddy grabbed him by the throat and slam dunked him on the concrete floor of the garage. From that day on, Slurp would walk a wide circle around him and would growl any time Daddy took a step or made any motion.

He wanted my brother and me to have a normal life, so he told us a little as possible. Years later, the truth would slip out. When Dr. King was killed, the school district wanted my brother and me taken out until things cooled off. Father told the principal that we were in school to learn. That if anything happened to us, he knew where a certain person lived.

His sons were not the source of any problem, so there shouldn't be any problem. End of discussion.

*****

Once, during the 1976 spring break from college, I took a walk through my old stomping grounds. I had not walked one block, when a police car started to follow me. I walked another block, the police car keeping pace. Finally, the cop pulled up next to me.

"Hey, what are you doing? Who are you?"

"I'm William Lucas. I'm just walking around."

"You the mailman's son?"

"Yes."

"You're okay then." He pulled off.

Eleven years in the area and the only thing that allowed me to safely walk in town was the fact I was the mailman's son.

We did not get an allowance. The way to get money was to clean out the mail car, collect all the loose change, and skim some off the top, or go on some errand and not bring back any change. One could go directly and ask Daddy for the money, but this was always traumatic. One found him working or sleeping. Believe me, you did not interrupt him while he worked.

I would enter the darkened bedroom to wake him up. Perhaps seeing him for the first time face to face in a week, I'd ask for money. He would ask how much I wanted, think about it awhile, say yes, then tell me to take what I needed out of his pants pocket. He would roll over and fall fast asleep.

If I needed two dollars, I might find three in his pocket. If I needed five I might find seven. He never refused me, but I never left without feeling bad about what he might have to do without, so I could go to the show and buy popcorn.

It was he, not my mother, who would stay up until I returned home from a night out. As I pulled into the driveway, I would see his shadow get up and go to the bedroom. Slurp would greet me, the TV would be still warm, yet Daddy would deny ever watching it. I might get in at 3:00 a.m., Daddy might have to get up at 4:00. He always claimed to have gone to bed at 9:00.

*****

An older Slurp became a different dog, more protective and attentive at the same time. He would only go after someone when he had backup (someone behind him); and he no longer liked to ride in the car or leave the boundaries of our land. Slurp became restless and anxious when the family was not a complete unit.

He knew what time each person should be home, he would go to the window about ten minutes before Daddy was due in, wait until he arrived, rush to the door and growl at him. With the rest of us, he would rush up and wait to be petted.

Each night he made rounds to each of our rooms. Each morning he was at the bedside of each person at the time they usually arose. He was better than an alarm clock, the only problem being Slurp couldn't tell the days of the week.

Slurp needed an article of our worn (couldn't be freshly washed) clothing to sleep on. He loved to play tug-of-war with socks. He would hide socks all over the house, to save for the times he wanted to play. And as time went along he would allow only me to pick him up.

Daddy grew increasingly irritated at this dog, searching any excuse to get rid of him. When Slurp's heart started to fail, it was I who paid the bills for the vet. When Slurp died, Daddy bought another dog, a cross between a real and a toy Chihuahua that we called Barf.

Barf picked up many of the habits that Slurp had. He waited by the same windows at the same times. Barf even had a run in with Daddy. While still a puppy, when Daddy was in bed with his bad back, Barf jumped on the bed and spilled hot soup all over him. Barf got the beating of his life.

Perhaps because this happened at a young age, Barf came to a sort of truce with Daddy. He would accept food from him but

Barf never again leaped on anything. He would have to be lifted up.

Not wishing another displeased pet, Daddy was forever trying to bribe Barf. Barf got to be one fat Chihuahua.

I named Barf. I don't know who named Slurp. I just tried to keep the tradition going.

Unlike Slurp, who would rest when everyone was home, Barf was always on edge and would bark at the slightest noise.

If Daddy had his way, no pets would have been allowed. However, as he did many times, he would put some views aside and considered the groups' wish.

*****

Released from the hospital Daddy attempted one more deal. He bought a new car. He tried to get loan insurance, but was told he was too old. (I have looked at the form, it does not show that he was refused. It shows that he turned down the insurance).

He agreed on the price, but when he returned to the dealer with a check, the dealer tried to switch cars on him. He was told that the car they had talked about had been sold. It had been sold they said, because Daddy had refused to put down any money on the car. Daddy said he never had put down money on a car in his life and wasn't going to start now. He told the dealer to get him another car. He said:

"There used to be something called trust. I say I want a car. You say you will sell me one. I give you money, you give me a car. When I say I'll be back for a car, I will be back for the car. My word is my down payment."

Since Daddy wanted a certain shade of blue, the car had to be ordered from another dealer. The salesman had to use his own money for the down payment. When the car came, we noticed it had set on a lot for 10 months. Daddy wanted a discount for the trouble of having to go back to the bank and having the paper work reflect different serial numbers. Daddy lost every round. He did not get the car he wanted. He paid more than what he wanted to pay. He did not get his discount. His time was running out, so he took the car.

He rode in the car to and from radiation treatments. He never drove it, not once.

Chapter five

What kind of fool am I

Jason and I are one year apart, opposite sides of the same coin. What came between us was not a case of sibling rivalry gone sour. The rift between us was over survival.

In the time of Martin Luther King, Jr., there was a philosophy known as non-violence, before black power, before black is beautiful, a time when we were still Negroes. One is either a coward or committed to the cause, when you allow somcone to spit on you. We were committed to the belief that change could only come through non-violence. Being human, we sold oursel-ves short to gain some peace. I became a clown, Jason did peoples homework. You do no have to be black to seek solutions to belong.

When Jason went black in high school, he was a moderate militant. I was a militant moderate. This translates to Jason having a big Afro and dressing in the style of militants. Jason felt that actions spoke louder than words. By looking black he made his statement. I dressed to avoid trouble, I wanted to look safe. I felt my words were my actions. Because I wanted no trouble, I believed when trouble came there could be no retreat. Jason, being with real militants, was invisible. I, being with whites, was always in harms way.

Jason spent one year longer in the old school district, one year less at Cherokee Springs. Friends he knew from nursery school through fourth grade, had a four year gap before seeing him again. They were able to find one another and check things out.

I spent one year less (up to the third grade) in the old school district, one year longer (five) at Cherokee Springs. when I reached Boone High, none would claim to remember me.

It was like the story of the fox who chewed off a foot to escape. I lost a leg and was given an artificial one, but at a distance everything looks the same. The new leg supports me, and enables me to function. The new leg, however, is not part of me. I do not know a time without Jason. When I lost his friendship, I lost my childhood. I could not think of those years, none of them...he was in each day. There was not a moment of joy he was not a part of; to hate him then was to forget all that was.

Had friends from before the move accepted me, I would have gone black as well. I would have gone white if my skin would have allowed it. I was forced to be William Lucas. So I became *William Lucas*.

Memories

During a baseball game, I hit a sure home run. The right fielder chased and threw the ball to the cut off man, at which point the gym teacher (high school baseball coach) who was in left field, yelled to have the ball thrown to him. So out the ball went into left field. I was thrown out at the plate.

*****

English teacher offers anyone willing to read *War and Peace* a pass on doing any other book reports for the entire year. I read *War and Peace*, but was unable to convince the teacher of this fact.

*****

English teacher assigns research paper. I am given F. Scott Fitzgerald. I write what I consider to be a terrific report, describing the man as a drunk who wasted his talent; a man who drove his wife insane. I concluded that most of his work was commercial garbage. I received a C+. F. Scott Fitzgerald was her favorite author. She felt that I put too much credence in the biography of his wife, and that I had selected the wrong critics in my research.

*****

English teacher tells everyone that they may do any sort of project that reflects their talents, writing, drawing, music, anything. I work three weeks on a painting. I bring it to class. She laughs at it. To get even, I invent a project. I present a history of jazz. I make up every word as I go along. I get an A.

*****

During my four years in high school, I could not get one English teacher to treat my writings seriously. I had to go to other teachers for advice. Freshman year it as a biology teacher. Sophomore year my German teacher (I would translate my jokes into German and tell them each day in class).

*****

When my *War and Peace* review was rejected, I submitted a review of *Moby Dick*. I got an A. I did not read *Moby Dick*.

*****

For drivers education, we had an instructor who gave directions like: "Turn right here left."

This instructor treated us as if we were his personal drivers. We would pick up his cloths at the cleaners and take him to various stores for shopping. In return he would bribe us with free pop and ice cream. During the driving sessions he would lay a pillow down on the seat and practice blackjack. He also let it be known that if anyone flunked the written portion of the test, a fifth of any good liquor could turn that into a passing grade.

*****

In life, certain patterns repeat themselves to the point we begin to take them on faith. If you ask someone what time is it, you expect to be given the correct time. At a baseball game, it is natural to hand your money over to a stranger who in turn passes it down a line of strangers to the vendor. Not only will the money reach the vendor, but your food and correct change will be returned to you.

Let's say you go into ten restaurants. At each you are given poor service, the food is burnt or under cooked. You are always seated in the worst table; have a hard time getting the attention of a waitress. Each time you complain you are told to go to some place that serves your kind.

Let's say that these are the first ten white owned restaurants you have ever entered. What is to prevent you from thinking that all white owned restaurants will treat you poorly?

At restaurant 11, you decide to demand your rights as a paying customer. You decide this even before the restaurant has a chance to show you any service at all. Restaurant 11 may in fact have intended to treat you to the best table in the house. However, your attitude is such that they give you the worst. You go away believing that restaurant 11 is just like the previous 10. Restaurant 11 thinks it just dealt with a jerk.

Restaurant 12 is going under. It treats all of its customers poorly. At restaurant 12 you think: here we go again. Not realizing that restaurant 12 is not bigoted...restaurant 12 is just a rotten restaurant.

Without a positive point of reference, one develops a different truth of what is. In 1965, we were met with out-and-out hate for the months of April, May, June, July and August. People drove to our house to scream obscene things at us. People called our house to tell us we were not wanted. People came to our door to ask us to move. For five months we had only one view of white people in our new town, all of it negative.

When school started, we were outsiders and different. Students everywhere are hostile to outsiders and to anyone different. In our eyes this just seemed to be a continuation of the previous five months.

By the time we overcame the natural hostility of our peers, we had an attitude problem (as least I did), which prevented us from realizing we were accepted until long after the name calling stopped.

After five years, I was primed and ready for disaster. When I was slapped that first day in high school, my defenses rushed up. I felt: "This is what you get when you trust people."

*****

Imagine running a race, a 50 yard dash; but your lane is the only one with a high hurdle. You can still win the race; you just have to try a lot harder. Racism is nothing more than an additional hurdle in life. Everyone has obstacles to over come, discrimination just adds a few more. The problem is when you lose sight of what are natural obstacles; vs. those that are self-made.

*****

One day I went on a job interview. I stand 5 feet eight inches tall and wear glasses. I had a fresh hair cut, and a brand new three piece suit. The first question asked:

"If you get this job, will you coach the basketball team?"

*****

A high school votes to have its prom at a local country club. Assumptions have been made. This particular high school has a handfull of black students. For the first time, these minority students are attending the prom. At the country club door, no black student is allowed to enter.

*****

While in college I take part in a self-study and assigned to a committee to see how other colleges handle their student problems. We travel to an elitist school in Wisconsin that considers itself the "Harvard of the Midwest." The school has one of the highest academic records for small schools in the country. It also has the highest suicide rate.

Everyone I meet at this school rushes up to me and wants to shake my hand. They ask me what position I play.

*****

On the way to work, my car breaks down. As luck would have it, I am near a tire places that does car repair. It is 7:00 a.m. and they open at 7:30, so I am first in line. I am low on cash. No problem says the manager, "We can get you an instant line of credit. All you have to do is fill out this form and we phone it in."

The form is filled out at 8:05 a.m. The credit clerk makes his phone call, I wait.

Between 8:30 and 12:30 I check back with the credit clerk six times for an answer. He has none. At 1:00 p.m. the manager comes over to ask why I am hanging around in his lobby. At 1:05 we take a visit to the credit clerk. The manager calls the instant credit people who in turn inform him that my credit had been approved since 9:05. The credit clerk claims he must have missed the call.

*****

Driving cross country to Denver on I-80, my brother and I stop for gas at a major rest stop. We are on fumes and pull into the gas station, wait for service. (Back then it was considered unsafe to pump your own gas). Twenty minutes pass before service is given. We go in for a bite to eat, 45 minutes to get a menu and when the food comes, it is burnt. I hand the money to the cashier but she just stares at me as if I don't exist. Finally, after a few moments of holding the money out, I let it drop and exit.

*****

At a Jr. High lunch room in 1969, a friend sits down next to me and exclaims. "Those damned niggers." Notices me, "Oh, hi William."

In a college dorm room in 1976, the door burst open, a girl exclaims, "Those damned niggers, won't let me watch *The King and I*. Notices me, "Oh, hi William."

Patterns.

I apply for a job at a major corporation. The interview goes badly and I leave. I am later contacted by the personnel office of this corporation (they contact me, not I them) and the personnel officer tells me that based on his information and my job qualifications, I have a good case for discrimination action.

All I needed to do was say the word. I say, "I don't want or ever hope to need a job that bad." I hang up and stay unemployed for five additional months.

*****

On my way to a party, I have a little trouble finding the correct address. I pull into a drive way. As I attempt to read the numbers on the door, the lady of the house demands to know what

I am doing. I try to explain. She thinks I am planning to rob her. I try to explain where I am going. She threatens to call the police. I make a hasty retreat next door. I was off by one house. At the party this lady calls to make sure I am who I said I was.

*****

While in college I stay up all night watching a stupid movie and at class the next morning I am red-eyed and a little listless. The teacher calls me aside.

"Are you on drugs?"

I say, "No. I was up watching a movie."

The teacher gives me a knowing nod.

"Come on, you can trust me. Are you on drugs? I'm cool."

*****

There is a small Catholic college in Joliet called the College of St. Anthony. I do not know where I would be if I had not gone there. After nine years of racial tension I found a place in which race is secondary. At this college I was faced with bigotry, but it is a pebble and I hardly notice.

I began to grow, to find self-worth. I discovered that my perceptions were false. I began to understand that some of my problems were self-created.

At college I wrote a play set in an insane asylum. Among the cast was a reasonable black man (which was why he was committed), a white person who thought he was black (he went around trying to convince people to become honorary niggers, become a minority instead of a Token). There is also a character known as the Bigot who made a speech about joining the Klan.

Bigot: I am here today, my friends, to tell you why you should join my team. The reason, my friends, is because the Klan can. The Klan can save you from the darkness of a blacks mind. The Klan can keep this world safe for white babies. The Klan can save you. And you want to be saved, don't you?

Do you know who you want to be saved from? I'll tell you. From the spear chucker. From the jungle bunnies. The Klan can save you.

For too long my friends, for too long, the white man has allowed the black man to have his way. We let them move to the front of the bus. We let them use our toilets. Now they threaten to take over!

These are the times that trouble a white man's soul. We are being run over in blackness. It is time we fight back. It is time we rid our land of those folks that darken our soil. It is time all whites should raise their hands united. White power! White power! White power!

It is time we kick those black asses off welfare and back into the cotton fields where they belong. The Klan can! By joining the Klan you will only be doing the blacks good. They need to be told what to do. They are just lost children who need help and direction. The Klan can give them what they need.

When you join the Klan, not only will you get a clean white sheet, a clean white hood, but all the good all-American vanilla white ice cream you can eat. This is a limited time offer. You get an autographed copy of the Klan book on the ten best ways to burn a cross.

By joining the Klan, you will help bring us closer to a world where all white children are free of association with a lesser race. Join the Klan. The Klan can!!

*****

Except for the part about ice cream, I was told that I wasn't that far from the truth in describing a hate rally.

*****

When Harold Washington became the first black mayor of Chicago, one of my fellow office workers became worried.

"I hear he plans to round up all the white people and put them into ghettos."

*****

The year of elections, 1968; big joke of that year, "I hear Sammy Davis Jr. is running in Alabama."

"What for?"

"The state line."

*****

Voice of America sponsors a contest in which high school students compete for scholarships by writing speeches. I competed and I won. I went to have a professional recording made of my winning speech, then waited for the district competition to take place. My sponsors came to me with bad news. My speech had been disqualified. It was not listened to, not judged...the machine had just been turned off.

"Why?" I asked.

In order to keep favoritism or discrimination out of the contest the speeches were to be nameless voices. My tape had my name on it.

"No one told me. I just read the speech the way I was told to write it."

"You should have read the directions," was all my sponsors had say. They were right, I should have read the directions.

I was so angry that I refused my certificate of achievement and my savings bond. I over ruled my father and said I was not going to the banquet that honored all the winners from the various high schools. I stayed angry. I vowed never to trust people again.

The principal of Boone High was a smart man. He waited a full year until practice for the graduation ceremony. He made an announcement about my winning and asked that I come up and accept my reward. What could I do.

My responsibility to freedom

by William Lucas

Freedom is like a wild bird. Put it into a cage and it will die. But, let the same wild bird grow up caged and he will think that he is free. Until the day he tries to fly.

Laws are like cages. They do basically the same thing. Laws protect us, laws confine us. Although we are not wild birds, we do share some things in common.

Each of us does not like to have our sense of freedom threatened. Wasn't it two hundred and ten years ago that our forefathers felt their personal liberty was in danger?

When England, the mother country, tried to enforce the Navigation Acts, the Sugar Act of 1764, the stamp act, plus many more.

It was the enforcement of the Navigation Acts that laid the seeds that would later sprout into a revolution. Don't you see? Freedom is nothing more than an abstract ideal. Laws that represent ideals about freedom can become outdated in time. As reality changes, rules that once protected freedom can limit freedom.

The time has come for all Americans to look deeply into themselves. Sing the *Star Spangled Banner* and mean it. Not just a prelude to a ball game. Our real responsibility to freedom is to the freedom of those yet unborn. They do not know what it is like to be free. They must have the chance to grow up free. They cannot be allowed to live in a land of oppressive laws and think that they are free. One day...one of our children might want to read a book, look at a piece of art or disagree with someone. And on that day...discover...they are in a cage...to stay.

Chapter six

Cause and effect

That first month we still had hope. He gained weight and was able to walk short distances. Like a dream, in the morning you wake up and it fades too quickly.

In the presence of my father I felt safe. I knew of no more a comforting sight than his face. As long as his mind still thought, he was my father. If he had lost both arms, legs and had his face disfigured, I would be proud to be seen in his company. That is not to say life with him was perfect.

I learned early that if I asked him to mail something he did not agree with, it did not get mailed. I found comic book subscriptions, requests for catalogs stuffed in drawers, or buried in his mail car. If I received something that in any way resembled junk mail, it was treated like junk. Once I wanted to enter a play writing contest. I sent away for the instructions. By the time I found the rules and application in the trunk of his car, I had already missed the dead line.

Out of frustration, I began to track all my mail. I would note when I mailed something, note when I received a reply. I would compare when my canceled check stamp against the day my order was shipped. I read each post mark with care.

I started to send for things, just so I could track them. Coins were cheap and you could send for them in every state of the union. I knew cut-off times for deliveries. I learned that mail placed in certain boxes were consistently a day slower than other mail boxes.

At first, I suspected my father of holding up my mail. Then I started to track his mail and my mothers. On the average, our mail took a week longer than necessary to reach us. This was not true for bills, only on request to government officials. Daddy was always in contact with people in Washington, D.C. I found gaps of five days between the post mark, the date of the letter and the time it reached our hands.

Once, I wrote to the CIA for an application. When the application arrived, it had been opened and resealed. One thing about the CIA, when they reject you, you get your original copy back. Much is made of this fact that no record of your submission is kept. I wonder if they think you never heard of a copier.

The same was true for my application for the FBI. You swear never to divulge the contents of the written exam. On the non-written portion you are handed a gun and told to pull the trigger as many times as possible in five minutes. After decades of playing the saxophone and typing on a manual typewriter, I had tough fingers. At the end of five minutes I slowed down more because everyone else was, rather than as a result of my finger getting tired. The trigger finger is the same as a trill key finger on the saxophone. In my weak hand, I was the lone trigger puller at the end of the elapsed time.

Daddy had no reason to hold up his own mail, but as far as the post office was concerned, Daddy was a trouble maker; a whistle- blower, a harmless eccentric or a dangerous crack pot. He had been trying to get someone to sue the post office for twenty years.

Daddy thought he was finally getting a head of the game in 1968. He got rid of the '57 Ford and bought a brand new '67 Plymouth. He had it about four months and that's when he was hit from behind while putting a letter into a mailbox. The Plymouth was torn in half. My father was rushed to the hospital. At first they thought his back was broken.

The man who hit him was white, unemployed, on welfare and did not have insurance. As far as the police were concerned it was an open and shut case but the Federal Government thought otherwise.

Rural Route Carriers must drive their own vehicles on the job. Daddy had insurance on his car for personal use the government is its own insurance company. Because this happened on the job, Daddy's insurance would not cover the car. The man who hit Daddy, while obligated to pay was heard to say, "It wasn't my fault. I don't care what the court said. You can't get water from a dry well. I intend to stay dry as far as that spook is concerned."

Postal inspectors concluded that the car lacked proper identification as a postal vehicle. From then on he had on top of his car a sign "U.S. Mail" with lights that flashed when you stepped on the break). They also said that because one wheel was on the pavement of the highway, Daddy had not done all that was possible to avoid being hit. Therefore, the government was not obligated in any way to pay for the car.

Faced with paying for a car he did not have, unable to collect from the man who hit him nor to collect anything from his own insurance company, Daddy borrowed against the house to pay for the car and buy a new one ('68 Plymouth). Then he sued his insurance company saying that he paid for uninsured motorist coverage which got him dropped from the company. He sued the man who hit him. It would be seventeen years before he finally settled for 1/3rd of the judgment. After the lawyers took their cut, he had $700. He tried to sue the Post Office stating that he was not at fault in the accident, that it made no difference what-so-ever if the guy who hit him knew he was hitting a postal vehicle. He had been hit doing official duties. The Federal Government decides who and for what they can be sued.

The first lawyer he hired to sue the Post Office accepted the retainer, then did nothing. Daddy sued the lawyer and got him disbarred. The next lawyer took his money, looked into the issue and said that he was sorry, it was too big a case for him to handle.

Daddy tried to get the governor involved. He contacted his Senator and Congressman and anyone that would listen to his story. The amount of money in question was only $5,000, but enough to bring him to the brink of bankruptcy. Had he kept the

Ford one more year, none of these events would have occurred. He would have had money in the bank and would have been able to buy a new car. He would have been mad at the Post Office, but he would not have gone to war with them.

Over the years, Daddy spent ten times the amount of money he wanted to recover. He would not let the issue drop and he was always finding new issues to continue the fight.

*****

A rural route carrier's salary is based on the length of his route and the number of stops he makes, called dismounts. In twenty years his route description never changed. The number of stops changed, but the description of his circuit (terms used to describe his job came from the days of Pony Express), never did. Daddy kept every piece of paper he was ever given at the Post Office. He had the route description for every year he had delivered mail. The date at the top changed, the stops changed. What streets he traveled, where he turned stayed constant, yet his route lost seven miles. He complained and it was determined that the previous years were wrong, and if he did not stop complaining he would owe the money he should not have received. Thus his salary was cut and retirement indirectly affected, since it is based on your highest three year salary.

Daddy sent things registered mail. Someone would sign for it, then the correspondence would disappear. One such letter was signed with the name of a federal official but the official said he did not sign for it. Daddy wanted the person who had signed the official's name prosecuted for tampering with the mail.

Lost in all this was the fact that the letter had disappeared. I could not convince Daddy that the issue was not who or who did not sign for the letter, the real question was, where was the letter. In his mind the letter he wrote was not important; that someone other than the official had signed was the only issue.

If you think this is petty, remember these two facts: 1) Postal worker delivering mail outside of Wrigly Field. A home run is hit. The postal worker catches the ball, shown on TV. The postal worker is suspended for leaving his mail unattended. 2) Postal worker places Christmas cards in the boxes of the people on his route. The postal worker is fired because he did not put stamps on the cards. When Daddy heard this, he began placing stamps on the cards he gave at Christmas.

The first address you are issued is yours to keep. Any changes that come later can only be done with your permission. That is why our house still has a Rural Route Post Box number. With a street address the police and fire departments can respond faster than to a rural route number. I know of three notices of address change that my father received. All of them refused in writing. You must refuse them or they go into effect. Daddy felt that when he needed the police in 1965, they couldn't find the place and there were only two houses to chose from. Let them stay confused.

Daddy went so far as to return any mail that came under the new addresses: "Return to sender. No such person. No such address."

I could never convince Daddy that these people did not know his history; that these people thought he was a nut.

"If I am, it is because they made me one."

*****

Cherokee Springs used our existence to gain federal grants and to brag that it was an integrated community. Jeffrey was taught at the new Junior High built with those grants, attending a racially-mixed school his entire time in Cherokee Springs. His world was not the world we faced. We paid the price of admission for something that should have been free.

By the time Jeffrey was born, the four of us had taken upon ourselves the burden of what had gone wrong. I felt that I must have done something to cause these people to dislike us so. I felt I was letting my father and all black children down. Any attempt to explain our fears to others just brought further grief.

"What did you expect? You put your children into that situation. You should have stayed where you belonged."

"Your husband would never have wanted such a fine house if you hadn't pushed him to it. He was just trying to give you what you wanted. You brought this on him. You brought this on your children."

"You kids don't know how lucky you are. You should get down on your knees and thank God for your parents. Look what they have done for you. What other parents would risk everything to give you a chance at a good education?"

"They deserve everything they get. Uppity bunch of niggers. Everyone of them."

"That light skinned wife of his thinks she's better than us. They always did have an easier time than us. They think they are something special. This will teach them."

After Robert Kennedy was shot, I had a secret fear. I felt I would come home one day and find that Daddy had been shot in the back of the head by a lone assassin.

That first year I developed a bad case of nerves. There were days I would do nothing but shake. Daddy would see this and tell me to stop. I would try, then I would start to cry. Daddy would demand that I stop crying. I would try. In time, I controlled my emotions and only shook in private.

When school started, my grades went into the ground. Not all of them, but a different subject each grading period. I could not take the stress. My new teachers could see I was trying hard, so they just concluded I was a little slow. It did not matter what my parents or old school had to say about me for, after all, my parents were parents. The old school had missed my poor eyesight and my speech problem, so it was felt that anything my old school had to say was suspect.

The speech class solved nothing. I could say any word with practice. It was no big deal to learn how to pronounce something in that class. I just stopped saying words that would be a problem. In time because no one heard any mispronounced words, my speech problem was considered cured. I thanked God for my thesaurus. My large speaking vocabulary was not reflected in my writing, since I was a poor speller, I only wrote words I could spell.

*****

I remember saying to my mother one night, "I want to go home."

"We are home," was her reply.

My parents always remarked that when I was small, I could not be shut up. Then I stopped talking.

I talked all day long at school. By the time I reached home I was exhausted. The problems my parents faced were so much larger than my own, I could not see the point of raising mine.

It was always known and expected that Jason would be the one to go to college. Jason did not work after school, he was expected to devote his time to academics and he did.

My problems with the move were known from day one. And like the kid who cried wolf once too often, my tears were seen as those of the crocodile. Jason took it like a man. Jason just took longer for the effects to show. The signs were there, but no one saw. I should have seen that Jason was fraying around the edges.

The C in gym. The illness. He took his drivers test, failed and refused to retake it. All these things were clues. It should not have been as big a surprise as it was. He graduated 7th in his class out of 753 and joined the Army as a private.

In a frustrated rage, Daddy demanded I find out what was going on with Jason. I had no answers and didn't really care. Years would pass before I was given a clue.

"I didn't think it was fair that you did not have a chance for college."

So as Jason felt himself drowning, he threw me a life line.

I accepted our parents dream of a son in college but I resented the pressure. I did not truly believe I could make it, nor did anyone else. Promises had been made through the years. If Jason did not want college, it was only fair that William go.

I chose a Catholic College. It was close to home if I didn't cut it, and most important of all, they had recruited me; the only college to do so). Daddy felt that one year at this college would put some sense into me. It did not.

When I announced that I would indeed return to St. Anthony's the following year, it was not met with the pleasure I expected. I had made the Deans list, had been a big success. Daddy had a problem about Catholics. So he saw his chance to kill two birds with one stone. I asked for advanced money to buy a used car to enable me to work two jobs that summer). Daddy thought he saw a way to bring Jason and me back together as brothers. His method was to tie us financially into a partnership. He offered a deal.

Instead of a used car, Daddy would put down money on a brand new car. I would make the payments that summer. Jason would take the car and make payments during the school years. Then we would trade off.

After the car was bought Daddy had to talk with me.

"This school you want to attend is more expensive than I counted on. After what I put down on that car...perhaps you better think of going to the state school."

Daddy misjudged me. He thought that if he could manipulate the car, he could bring me around on my choice of school by threatening to remove financial support. After nine years of hell, I was not about to risk my time in heaven. I told him I was going to return and stay until told to leave. I went to Jason and demanded he help me. I wish today I could say I asked him for help, but I demanded it of him.

A war of wills was on between Daddy and me. Jason blinked first. Jason drove our car off a mountain in Colorado. He was so drunk at the time that he didn't get a scratch. He did, however, total our car.

Once again Daddy demanded that I find out what was going on. This time I listened. This time, I felt I had let Jason down. I began to hate myself. From that day on my heart was not in college. I believed I had no heart. Jason continued to send money and declared that everything was fine. I did not believe him. I did not believe I would finish college. I started to cut myself off from people to get ready for the day I would have to leave.

As time went along, Daddy became proud of my degrees. He even bragged about how hard I had to work for them. When I needed him to co-sign for a car I wanted to buy, he nudged me toward a more expensive four-wheel drive Bronco, "In case you can't make the payments, I can use it on the mail route."

I had owned the car nine months (forty-one payments left) when I was laid off from work. I stayed unemployed for 6 months.

At my lowest point, when I didn't know if I could make the payment, I would not go to him for help. I still remembered college. Daddy had forgotten college. Daddy would forget years later why I bought the Bronco. When I told him I hated that vehicle, that I only bought it because I felt it was the only way he would co- sign, it was like I had hit him with a two-by-four. He wanted to be mad at me, then his eyes grew sad.

"I would not deny you anything."

"I know that. I just don't always believe it."

*****

My basic problem with Jason stemmed from a similar incident when I went to him for help and he refused me. Then years later when he pretended that he and I were not related, I became cold as ice.

My high school sweetheart became a casualty, when she explained why she had almost not gone to the prom with me. I could never forgive this temporary lapse in faith.

Before the move I believed in Santa Claus and Oz. By the time I left high school, I trusted no one, forgave no one, and never gave any one a second chance to hurt me.

I wish someone could explain to me how a person who finished seventh in his class could graduate without a full scholarship somewhere. Colleges were begging for academically-strong black students. At least, that was the rumor.

Someone in that high school should have been there for Jason. Someone should have gone to our parents wondering why a college bound student was not applying for or being accepted any where. Advise should have been so easy that Jason could never have thought that his attendance to a college would impact on my ability to go.

Jason fell through the cracks.

In my four years at Daniel Boone, I had five different counselors. Each was lucky to match my social security number to my name, let alone my face.

Daniel Boone High School was not in the business of education when we were there, it was trying to survive. The school had money trouble, the state was threatening to close the place. There were too many students in a building built during the depression.

Many of us suspected a ploy on the part of the school board. A plot to outrage the parents, that when a vote for more money came up it would have to pass. Class time was cut. Time between classes was reduced. The school day was split in two. Extra activities were curtailed, except for sports.

The first shift (1-5) ended at 11:30. For this reason it was felt no one needed a lunch break. 6th period was set aside for those interested in extra courses or events, the newspaper, or clubs, and 7-11 was the late shift.

Splitting the shifts not only allowed the same sized school to hold twice the students, it was seen as a way to reduce racial tension. The balance of students was 50-50, it became 70-30 per shift. We used to say the difference was between day and night; black and white. The early shift was the brighter shift. This shift was filled with those students who had vested interests (sports, college bound, music). Busses left at the end of 5th, 6th, and 11th periods. This is where I fell through the cracks.

To take jazz band, I had to take regular band. Being in regular band gave me 6 periods worth of classes. Being in jazz band gave me 7 periods. This was true for all members of the two jazz bands, and for the members of the various choral groups. We all fell into the pit of faulty logic.

If we wanted to participate in music, we would have to go 7 complete periods without a break. There were no busses at the end of 7th period either. Later after complaints, two busses were found to take over 100 kids home to seven separate communities. Music classes, by tradition, met first period and the music teacher refused to move either the regular groups or the special groups into the 6th period.

The policy of Daniel Boone High was that during the first week of school nothing, no problem, not one thing would be discussed. You were expected, told, forced, to put up with whatever problem that first week.

When the schedules were printed, music was expected to place its courses into the 6th period. At some point the music department won the battle to stay in the first period. For reasons unknown, all students who wanted to participate in the special groups found something else in the 1st period slot.

The question became, which class to attend. Since I had gym on my schedule listed 1st and 7th, I saw no real problem in just going to 1st period music. I went to my gym teacher to try and explain.

"That paper say you in my class?"

"Yes."

"Then get in line."

"I'm not going to be in your class. Next week..."

"I don't want to hear any excuses. Get in line."

The next day, I went to band to explain why I was not there. The band instructor said to stay. I did. When the week was up, I and some other lucky people went to the registrars office to straighten out the paper work. We thought everything was fine.

When the first report cards came out, I was listed as having 23 days absent. Students ranged from 7 to 45. I was in trouble until I explained what had happened. I again trucked to the registrar's office. I then had to go to my teacher and have him make copies of his attendance book to prove I was indeed there. By the time all was said and done, I could account for all but two of the days in question.

The school refused to correct the record completely. They turned my 23 days absent to 21 days tardy. At this point I had not missed a single day at school. People with perfect attendance were given white Sox tickets, silver dollars and stuff. I felt cheated out of my good name. I did not like the fact that my official record would forever show me late to classes when I was not late. I was not alone, but it did not make me feel any better.

Not a one of us had been contacted about an abnormal amount of absences from school. None of our parents had been called to explain why we were not there. We suspected that the reason our records could not be changed was that our records did not reflect reality. And school officials could not afford to answer questions.

In gym class, one had to wear approved gym clothes; shirt, shorts, jock, white socks and shoes. If you were unable to appear properly dressed, you could rent any article you needed for 25 cents. Each item was dyed pink to discourage theft. My freshman year, I took a red magic marker and wrote my name in large letters on each side of my shoes to prevent them from being stolen. They were. Two years later, I had to rent a pair of shoes. I was given a pink pair. I could still read my name but I made no effort to claim them.

Remember the show "Welcome back Kotter", about a bunch of high school sweat hogs. Because Daniel Boone was on split shifts and circumstances forced me into the late shift, I took a sweat hog course.

The course had a real name, but it existed for one reason. In the state if Illinois, you must pass a test on the U.S. Constitution in order to obtain a diploma. This class existed to get you through that test. The test was mandatory and only a few classes gave it. Points were given for attendance (60% of your grade was attendance). We all knew that if you passed the constitution test it didn't matter if you flunked the course, you could still get your diploma. We all knew that if you got an A in this course, but failed the constitution test you weren't going anywhere.

In this class was a star basketball player on academic probation, students I thought of as losers and me. Out of boredom, I helped the basketball player get through the class, which was very important to him. I cared about my grade point average, and with attendance being 60% of my grade, I showed up at every class. In time I realized that I was the real fool in the room.

These non-college track students were more open and forgiving in the nature of people than anyone in the advance classes. Once I got over my superior attitude I became an accepted member of the group.

The following year, when the basketball player became a key player in our drive toward a state basketball championship, the Big H, as he was called, taught me an important lesson. The day before the big game, there was a pep rally. As the Big H. was waiting for his name to be called, he saw me in the crowd, came over and he shook my hand just as his name was called and the spotlight hit us both. For a brief moment, I basked in the glory of his time in the sun.

*****

Daniel Boone was a school that resembled a castle, complete with a tower. All it needed was a moat. It was impossible to go from the fourth floor tower to a corner first floor room in the five minutes allotted between classes. Many of us felt we were running the three-minute-mile every day of the week. You had to cheat to even have a chance. One would pack up before class ended and wait for the bell like a starting pistol. Teachers knew that when the bell sounded the class was gone and they were told not to allow students into class late without a pass. One student was sent to detention for arriving late to German class. He could not travel the distance in time, so he was late everyday and written up for it every day.

Daniel Boone was known as an open school at that time which meant that you could enter and exit the school at will. The only controls were that no one was allowed in the hallways between classes without a pass, and no one was allowed into a class after the bell without either a pass or punishment. Students who couldn't get to class on time could walk across the street to the shopping center or face a detention for being late.

Bathrooms were always a problem for one had to know what crowd owned which bathroom before you entered. Each was a hangout for a certain gang or group. There were a few safe rooms, but pity the fool who entered the wrong one.

This does not mean that teachers did not teach, counselors did not counsel or that students did not learn. You had to work real hard if you did not fit the pattern.

If you took classes and were on the day shift, you were out of school by 11:30. You could have an afternoon job, see anyone you wanted 6th period, then walk, or take the bus home.

If you were on the night shift, you could sleep late, go shopping or do your homework in the early morning and work nights. If you had to see someone, you could make your way to the school early. It was good for the students who fit the pattern.

That small group who did not walk to school, did not have access to a car and who wanted to participate in extra classes, found that access was something that had more to do with luck, than with right.

Worst of all Daniel Boone fostered the feeling that certain things meant more than others. The band room, with all those expensive instruments, leaked and it was not repaired. When the field house developed a leak, it was repaired the next day. It was important to maintain the confidence of athletes, keeping them up and competitive. Little effort went toward the academic; no one went around saying, "If you've got the basics, you can do it. You can compete with any one."

I took a college writing course and we were asked to write an original paragraph. I wrote:

> To understand the difference between a Whatsamacallit and a Thingofmajig, you must first understand the difference between a what and a thing. They are so close as to be almost interchangeable. A *what* usually refers to inanimate objects given human characteristics, like a car. so the difference between a whatsamacallit and thingofmajig, is very like the difference between a Volkswagon Bug and a Vokswagen Beetle.
>
> (Excerpt taken from the Lucas book: *Worthless Information*)

For this I received a big F circled in red with the line stating: "I said original paragraph."

I went to the teacher and said that this was an original paragraph, that I didn't think many people had tried to define the difference between a whatsamacallit and a thingofmajig. He pointed to the line referring to the book excerpt. I said there was no such book, that my name was Lucas, that I was the author of *Worthless Information* He did not believe me, but gave me a D for effort.

Without confidence to back up one's efforts, there can not be success. The teacher with a Harvard degree, said original, I turned in something original. I could not believe the grade I received. By the time I left that school, I was convinced my scores did not reflect me. Jason must have been as convinced of the lack of value of his 3.97 GPA.

In mid August, Honey called to tell me Daddy had to return to the hospital. On the way home, I purchased a new suit to wear at the future funeral.

Chapter seven

The mountain top

My mother was a September bride. I have not talked much about her for the story of the black woman has been told often. We have heard of them striving against impossible odds to raise their children. We have not heard of the fathers who stayed, the black males who would not give in to pressure and leave responsibilities behind. When I was small she spanked me. I grabbed hold of her, crying. Thc harder she hit, the harder I held on not to lose her.

That September was their 39th together. On the way to radiation I broached the subject with Daddy.

"Today is your wedding anniversary."

"I forgot."

"Do you want me to get something?"

"Yes."

"What?"

"Flowers."

"Do you think you can sign a card?"

"I'll try."

I went to the gift shop and I bought two dozen long-stemmed roses and a vase. I read him the card. I waited and watched as struggled to write his name and two words.

"With Love."

Honey was happy. Daddy thought it a bit much.

As he neared the end, I searched my mind for good times we had together. Daddy thought of the times he had taken Jason and me with him as helpers to work on people's houses as special moments. I thought of them as torture. I had gone to be with him, but once there I quickly tired of pulling nails from wood, sweeping floors and carrying supplies. While Jason continued to work, I would find a place to hide.

The Christmas after the move he gave me an expensive gift, one of the first Polaroid cameras. I had not asked for it, nor had I any interest in photography. He wanted me to have it, an extra special gift, that I had not earned or needed.

At some point we just got out of sync with each other. He owned an army surplus Underwood manual typewriter. From the day I found it, I fell in love with it. I felt such a sense of accomplishment typing a page. Hitting the return carriage became an art. I would pound the keys in time with music, thinking of each keystroke as a musical note. I would make different sounds with how much pressure I put on each key. I took this twenty pound typewriter to college with me and called it my portable. My last year in college I was presented with an electric typewriter.

I got up Christmas morning, opened the box, saw the typewriter, I headed back to bed. My mother told me I had disappointed her husband. He had expected me to type something. "You don't understand," I said. "I'll have to give up using the Underwood."

I didn't like that electric. The ribbons cost $7.00 each, the Underwood used $1.00 ribbons that rewound until the ink faded away. Once with the electric and that was it. I used a new ribbon on the underwood for my final draft and I used the old ribbon for rough and unimportant work. The electric hummed preventing me from listening to music and typing at the same time. I was happy and sad. I was about to graduate and then I get a typewriter.

As far as the Federal Government was concerned, Daddy was born in 1922. I had known he lied to get into the Army, but I never thought about what had to be done to convince the military of this. Going through his papers I found a request that a birth certificate be issued. It stated the circumstances of his birth and

and on the back was a sworn statement from Daddy's mother confirming that she gave birth in 1922, to a girl.

The certificate had been corrected to reflect male. It was too late to get the story for Daddy's ability to concentrate was almost gone. He only wanted to go home. Arrangements were made, We took him home.

At the house he wouldlie in bed and look at the walls. I was checking on him, when he called me over to his side.

"I lied," he said.

"About what?"

"The Army. I was not operated on for my back."

He had often told the story of working on a truck, having the support fall and pinning him under it.

"I want you to know the truth. I was operated on for varicose veins."

I started to suspect he wasn't all there.

"After the bombing...(He had never said anything about being in an air raid before)...the doctor kept making me tell the story over and over. He promised to get me out early. I lied about my injuries. Said I never had any. Thought if told...truth...would keep me in...I just wanted out...wanted you to know...truth."

I checked his discharge papers. Honorable discharge 1944; 25% disability, varicose veins. He was listed as a truck driver. He said he never was near the front lines. I remembered all his talk of cover ups and conspiracies. Friendly Fire?

The first claim made on the homeowner's insurance was to replace the picture window damaged by the BB gun. A small crane was needed to lift the window out and place the new one in.

The second, third and fourth claims were for the flower boxes There was no fifth claim from this insurance company. They dropped us after the fourth. With stone left over from the house, Daddy built four flower boxes that lined the entrance and exit of the circle driveway.

One of the boxes demolished. Daddy believed he could rebuild it for about $200.00. He contacted the insurance company and asked for $400.00. The insurance company balked and sent a man out to appraise the situation.

"Well," the appraiser said. "$2,000.00 should do it."

"Are you sure?" said Daddy.

"It's obvious you don't know much about this type of work. You may know landscaping, but who ever did the work on these boxes was a craftsman."

"Is that so," said Daddy.

"That's right. And to match the stone, to duplicate the pattern of the other three takes a qualified stone mason. Not many of those around any more. Tell your boss that I'm advising the insurance company to pay him just what he originally asked. Let it come as a surprise. Okay."

"Okay."

The insurance company offered Daddy $350.00. Daddy said the price was now $1,200.00. He got it. He spent about $50.00.

"You just have to think like it's a jig saw puzzle."

Those boxes were magnets. When the second one was knocked down, the insurance company paid to have the work done by some one else.

When the replacement window fogged up, Daddy demanded a replacement. The people who came to replace the replacement window, knocked down the box for the third time. At which point the insurance company told Daddy to go find insurance someplace else.

Sick of rebuilding the boxes, Daddy filled each one with concrete. A lady driving a Nova lost control of her car and drove into a ditch up and over one. Not much was left of the car, but the box was knocked down intact. It took three days to figure a way to pull it up and into position. He had to borrow a tractor from Mr. Brown.

After people think they are your friends, they tell you things that make you wonder:

"William, you're okay. I mean you Blacks. After all you are Christians. It's us against the Jews, right!"

"Hey, William? What's the black stuff between elephants' toes?"

"What?"

"Slow natives."

The first week at Cherokee Springs, some considered it the height of hilarity to shake my hand and say:

"I'm Lincoln, you're free."

I was given the telephone number for a White Supremacy group. I called and got this recorded message:

Rumor to spread for the day: "Jewish Doctors are infecting Black babies with AIDS." Remember, keep the Jew and the Black at each others throats. Let them kill each other off and save us the trouble.

Our enemy is not, repeat, not the Black Militant. They can be used. The Black Militant is after the same thing we are, they do not want mixing of the races and they do not like Jews. Let him believe we can work together. Their time will come later.

Contact you local chapter for tomorrow's number.

When Harold Washington was running for Mayor of Chicago, people were wearing color buttons, either white buttons, or black buttons. No lettering, no pictures, just color.

I was talking to a man who had come back from a seminar in which people learn to deal with a hostile press. During one simulated interchange he thought the following comments hilarious:

Question: Your company is responsible for dumping thousands of gallons of toxic waste on a public beach. What do you plan to do about it?

Answer: We plan to hire minorities, wrap them in cotton and have them roll along the beach to soak up the material.

Question: Won't that be hazardous to their health?

Answer: Not really. Studies show most of them will be dead from petty crimes long before symptoms can show.

I have also heard people say:

"The lighter the skin, the smarter the black."

"When freedom came, all those house niggers knew how to do was take orders."

"Religion is the White man's tool to control the Negro."

"How can you be proud of a slave name?"

I did not have to be told Daddy had returned to the hospital. I got into my car left work and drove home. In the parking lot I had closed my door and looked up into the face of Jason. Together, in sync for the first time since the '60's, we went to his room to wait.

Daddy taught me how to bowl with my right hand. I was left handed, but having his attention was enough not to mention it. He was always confused between Jason and me. Jason was the right handed one. We were bowling in a formerly restricted bowling alley. Daddy staged a protest to earn the right to spend money to bowl. There was one alley in Falcon Heights, and for years they refused Blacks the right to throw a ball down the lanes. As Daddy often said, "Pit greed against race. Greed wins."

Money allowed Blacks to bowl. Like the roller rink, Tuesday and Thursdays became Black nights. The rest of the time the lanes were white. Not by law, but by unwritten understanding.

At 3:00 a.m., Jason reacted to the lack of sound. I could still see his heart beat, I knew he still lived. I leaned over and whispered, "You did good. We will miss you."

A tear rolled down one eye and then he was gone.

Chapter eight

Haven't got time for the pain

Jason left to tell our mother. As I waited for their return, I combed Daddy's hair. I shut his eyes. I made things as neat as possible. He always wanted to look his best.

A cousin who lived upstairs from us before the move, was a nurse at the hospital that my father spent his last six months in and out of. So great was her concern that many in the hospital thought that Daddy was her father.

Being a decade older, she knew my father before Junior died. She knew my father when he was courting my mother. She knew him when he laughed and played the piano. "When he was normal," I heard her say.

Jeffrey was born when Jason and I were hurting our parents more than we hurt each other. Without Jeffrey I could not have found my way back from bitterness. He had the misfortune to look identical to me. Put our baby pictures side by side, and no one could tell them apart. He too, was left handed, and for some odd reason, he enjoyed my company. I could not leave the house without him wailing to come along. I was sixteen and pushed him away. Daddy asked me to give Honey a break and spend some time with the kid. I took him to the zoo. Along the way I noticed he was in some distress.

"What's the matter?"

"Tooth hurts."

"I better take you home."

"No! I want to be with you."

When he said that, I heard me. I could look in that face and see my own. Like the Grinch who stole Christmas, my heart grew a little. He was three when I went to college. He begged and begged to visit, so one weekend he came. That Sunday, when Honey picked him up, I overheard him tell her in amazement, "He was nice to me."

He came to see a play I was in. During the course of the show, my character was killed. Jeffrey had to be brought back stage to be shown I was still alive. The next night, as I was doing my death scene, a small voice rang out, "He's not dead. He's not. He's acting."

When I left Cherokee Springs, I was President of the Student Council. Daniel Boone considers itself to be a city. It elects a mayor and aldermen. Wishing to continue participation in Student Government, I looked up the district I was in and I discovered that as far as the city of Boone was concerned, I did not live in Cherokee Springs, I lived in East Falcon Heights.

Nobody wanted to live in East Falcon Heights. East Falcon was poor, black and crime laden. One drove through East Falcon with doors locked. In 1965, East Falcon had three gas stations. Today it has none. East Falcon has changed its name to Dodge Heights to improve its image.

I write these terrible things about the place, yet I went there every month for nineteen years to get my hair cut. Daddy remodeled houses there, and it was in East Falcon Heights that Daddy chose to establish a Masonic Lodge, which he named after a black surgeon who died in prison. I could work there, eat there, shop there, have my hair cut there, but East Falcon was on the wrong side of the expressway the last thing I wanted was to have my name associated with it. I pretended that my house was not where it was on the map, ran and won, as the representative of Cherokee Springs.

The house location was always a problem. That first summer, it was a prison. We did not set foot in the town until after we had registered. We could not tell our old friends about the move, so each day after school until summer, we were picked up by Honey and driven home. At home, where once we had upstairs relatives, friendly neighbors and a block to roam, it was now just Jason and me, our dog Slurp and one big pile of dirt to play on.

We exhausted every variation of two person games we could imagine. We played a sort of baseball. The pitcher would throw the ball and start running backward. The batter would hit the ball up as high and shallow as possible. If the ball was caught, you were out. When the ball was touched, you had to stay on the base you were at. If you were attempting to go home, the pitcher would try and hit you with the ball. If he did you were out.

We invented our own games. As cars went down the highway, we would give ourselves a certain lead and race the car to the end of our property line. One point for each car beaten. We would alternate on cars. The one with the most points was the winner.

One game used the telephone pole as a target. We would bat a baseball at sections of it, like a dart board. We played checkers, chess, Chinese Checkers, marbles, Monopoly, Clue, Life and Battleship. We got into major disputes. Once during a two week game of Monopoly (we had split evenly on the property, except I owned the only monopoly on the board) we had to take money from other games just to keep going. Since I had the only monopoly, I felt Jason should quit. After all, it was only a matter of time. He would not quit, nor would he agree to let the game be a draw. I got tired of it, picked the game up and threw it against a wall. It was the last time we ever played monopoly together. The pattern would repeat itself.

We bought a basketball baseboard and put it up over the garage. Daddy, however, objected to the marks left on the garage door when we missed the basket, he made us take it down. Jason took the baseboard to the back patio and placed it on the ledge of the patio wall, braced it somehow and spent a great deal of time doing nothing but shooting baskets. I felt it was stupid, and refused to play.

In high school, Daddy surprised us by buying a playground style pole and regulation baseboard. It was cemented in place in the ground opposite the garage. By the time, however, Jason and I were not on speaking terms.

That pole and board appeared seven years after the move; seven years after we had been promised a combination tennis/basketball/volley ball court. Daddy had set aside part of the land for our own playground. He had us level it, and go around with buckets to pick up all the rocks. Each year I waited for the dirt to become blacktop. I was unaware of the financial problem Daddy faced. I only felt let down.

Daddy always wanted the best; Half measures could not do. It was not enough to put a board over the garage. We needed the real thing. Adults can wait, but children grow up.

Although we were not the only children isolated in a rural area our isolation was greater out of fear for our safety. My first new friend was a person with a famous name, Jesse James, who was an only child, wore glasses and lived as far out as you could get and still be in the state. I was invited to his house; he had a real tree house. At that time our house was incomplete and visitors not welcome. We could not talk over the phone (what did kids have to say to one another) and were not in the same class grouping at school. There was only the bus and recess. It was just easier to find a new friend.

The street we lived on was used as a drag strip on weekends. People drove up and down yelling obscenities at us and tossing beer bottles on our front lawn. Each day for years, our lawn was littered with garbage. It became second nature to just clean it up.

The nearest store was a three mile round-trip walk. The town proper would have been eight miles. When I did make the walk, I would carry a rock because some people thought it was funny to swerve toward you, as a joke. Fear kept me from ever accepting a ride. When asked I would say I needed the exercise.

We were both tested. I needed glasses and had a speech defect. Jason was bright enough to be doubly promoted from the 4th to the 6th grade (declined).

Each grade had a letter group. For example 7A (7th grade group A) was considered the fast lane. A person in 7H was thought to be a little slow. This was compounded by the fact that recess periods were staggered and certain groups never came into contact on the playground. A 7A and 7H never had recess periods together. 7A's and 7B's had recess periods together. There was also the perception that certain teachers only taught certain letter groups. Jason was a letter A.

My letter group was for those who weren't slow or fast; we were the E's. We children could do better but, for some reason didn't ourselves. I discovered in 1967 what grouping meant. That year I took the music aptitude test and I scored a 63 out of 100, a D-. Within a week my parents received a letter expressing joy that their son displayed an ability toward music. They were invited to come down on band day, so that my musical aptitude could be brought to full flower.

Daddy believed playing a musical instrument was a good way to make contacts. Jason was playing clarinet. The teacher looked at me and said I was perfect for the baritone. To me the baritone looked like a miniature tuba; I did not like the size of it. So I said, "Ain't no way I'm carrying that thing around."

The teacher said my arms were too short for the trombone, how about the saxophone? That's how I became a saxophone player.

Band brought me into contact with people outside of my group, students who shared a common interest. Outside of that, I did not see them. To talk over a lesson, to check on fingering, I had to stand by their classrooms when their recess periods began, as mine ended, and talk as the shifts ended. This brought me into contact with teachers who were never my teachers.

One teacher who heard me express some views on life, said I was an old man in a boys body. He called me Pops and and I in turn, started to call him Sonny.

Sonny was the first teacher outside the classroom who would talk to me about anything I wanted. It was important to me and he always stood out in my mind for that reason.

When my high school jazz band toured the various Junior High Schools, I was looking forward to seeing Sonny again.

Sonny did not remember me! For the first time, I became aware that my view of the past was distorted.

I saw myself as singled out because of my color. I saw those days as just my brother and me, the rest white. I forgot about any other minority. I forgot about other people's problems.

A year ago, in a Dairy Queen one of the Hispanics from back then, asked me:

"How did you do it? They never seemed to bother you. Juan and I were always picked on. No one bothered you?"

She seemed a little bitter in her memory that my time was so easy, compared to hers. What was it that blinded us to each other? I though she was the one who had the easy time.

I believe that if your assumption in life is that people are basically good, no matter how deep the pit you may find yourself in, any excuse will do and you will start to drag yourself out. My first lasting friend back then had my same last name, only he spelled his with a K instead of a C, Sam Lukas. When attendance was called, we thought it funny to answer at the same time. Because we were L's, we were near each other in class. We started calling one another cousin. I would say he was the white sheep of the family. He would say that he was working on his tan so he could fit in better. On trips with his parents, I would pretend I was the son and he a distant relative. We found the looks people gave us the funniest thing in the world.

We invented conversations for people who like to listen to private talks.

"Say cousin. How dark do you think I will get this year?"

"Well, if you want to pass for Colored, you better get to work."

We would be laughing inside as the people, pretending not to be listening had eyes bulging out. It was a triumph when the whispering started.

Sam played the trumpet, a fact that kept us in contact throughout high school and that first summer before college. Sam could be described as a Geek or a nerd by today's standards. I just saw him as Sam. His interest tended toward electronics and for one science project he built a computer. We had two things in common; our last name and music. For nine 1/2 years it was enough.

I have been lucky that at the oddest moment I find someone who lifts my spirit. In high school, I never expected it to happen.

Boone High, in an attempt to make due, built an almost high school, called the Freshman-Sophomore building nine miles from the Boone High campus. This building lacked all the facilities of a complete high school. Students were shuttled by bus back and forth for certain sports and music programs. When I arrived it was known as the Freshman building.

Roaming the halls of the Freshman building was a student named Joe who lived two miles north of us, across the street from the bus station. He had the freedom to pick and choose which bus he wanted to take. Jason and I had to ride our assigned bus. Joe played the saxophone and was a year older than I. I thought of him as a jerk.

High school must have been tough on him as well. Set back a year his friends moved on to the main building. When I needed a friendly face, so did he. I wanted someone to talk to and so did he. We became friends.

For reasons unknown to me, and perhaps because of our house location, that first year my classes kept me away from the classmates at Cherokee Springs who had accepted me. Had I been with them, my transition would have been easier. First class of the day was math class with no one from Cherokee Springs in the class. Across the hall, an equivalent math class had nine students from Cherokee.

We had been taught by the same teacher, yet we were now in different class rooms. I rode the bus with them, then walked to a different room. The teacher of this math class did not like me hanging around his room yet he could do little about it because school had not officially started. The more hostile he became, the more I hung around class. Had he let me say hello to my friends, I would soon have stopped as I got to know more and more other students. He hated me on sight, and I stood by my rights.

He would not let me in the class room. I would stand outside the door and tell jokes to Sam and others. I waited until the warning bell and started to count down the seconds to when he could close the door. After two months, I wore him down.

This pattern repeated itself throughout high school. What started out as an innocent action would be mis-interpreted and I would refuse to allow myself to become stereotyped. It never occurred to this teacher that I had gone to school with these students. He thought I was some black kid hanging out where he didn't belong. It was an Algebra class and not many blacks were taking advanced math classes freshman year.

I was constantly told I looked like someone named Mark Kofelt. I had never seen or met this guy, yet that first year thirty people came to me to say how much I resembled him. I met Dan when he came to say I looked like Mark.

At college I was standing in the cafeteria line and there was Dan. I did not know he was attending St. Anthony's, nor did he know I was. Thus, someone I knew in high school became a friend in college. I was the best man at his wedding. Today he is a doctor.

A trademark of mine was to hold loud meaningless conversations with someone, just to upset bystanders who listen, but pretend they don't. People would pick up on this and strike up discussions. The president of St. Anthony's, Dr. Smith, approached me at a cocktail party. We were surrounded by members of the Board of Trustees, faculty and important alumni. He said,

"William, after you graduate we don't intend to let anymore blacks into this school."

You could have heard a pin drop and bounce in that room. Dr. Smith waited for my reply.

"Then who's going to wash your car? Shine your shoes?"

"We'll hire in."

"Can I get an application?"

As the tension relaxed you could hear people say how well Dr. Smith got along with my kind. They missed the point. They always do. Dr. Smith got along with students, period.

I got to know Jane from such conversations. She, Dan and I worked as student security guards at college. She liked the late shift, I worked the early, Dan worked a swing shift. Switch over was at 2:00 a.m., Dan was the outside man and would come inside at 2:50. Together we would wait until we heard Jane's steps on the stairs and begin.

"The secret is two flashes, wait a beat then one. UFO's never respond to the reverse."

"Now what angle would that be, 45 degrees?"

"No...angle is very important, 48 degrees. No more or less."

She would come down and often proclaim, "I don't understand!"

Today she understands. She's better at my game than I am. We were driving to Atlanta to visit Dan and his wife and we stopped at a diner to eat.

"Did you notice something odd?"

"What's that."

"All the cars have ugly license plates."

"Yeah, I noticed that too. Not good one's like Illinois."

"And the flags we keep seeing..."

"Yes?"

"Do you think we should tell them that it's red and white stripes, 50 stars on a blue background?"

"The next one we see... You do it."

"You do it."

"Tell you what, lets flip for it."

"I don't think so."

"Why's that?"

"Floor's dirty."

I have found that people need an excuse to be friendly. Driving across country, I got one of those inflatable dinosaurs and put him in the passenger seat with seat belt attached. More people waved and said hello at gas stations, than ever did before.

I didn't fit the pattern. A teacher wanted to teach me a lesson in high school when she caught me talking in class. She made me stand in front of class and told me to talk for ten minutes.

At the end of eight, she asked me to stop. I was having such a good time telling my jokes that she felt I wasn't getting the point.

In college, a teacher wanted everyone to know what it felt like to be ignored. So he said, "I want everyone in class to ignore William. I don't care what he says, ignore him."

I said, "Did you hear, they arrested Mr. Green for rape." Everyone turned their heads to listen.

When I recall those early years, I hold no resentment toward the children of Cherokee Springs. At nine, kids can be cruel, but it is the adults who feed the slurs with which I had problems. It goes on today, 1990. In Iowa, small town-rural America, the heart land, there is a white family who adopted a little boy from Brazil. This boy's skin tone marks him as an African-American in the eyes of the townspeople. This couple took their son to the park to play. He ran to the swings. As he pursued happiness, other children, with suggestions and encouragements from near-by adults began to taunt him with names like "Nigger, spook." When his parents stepped in to stop it, the adults wanted to know why they were ending the fun. Is this heaven? No, its Iowa.

Joe drove a Chrysler Station Wagon the way you would drive a race car. I made the mistake once of following Joe to a regional basketball game. He took every blacktop back road he could find at speeds of 80 to 90 miles an hour. I could keep up with him for I was in a double barrel, dual exhaust Thunderbird, but I didn't want to. One of his tricks was to let me get close to him, then he would turn on his lights. Seeing the rear lights glow, I'd think he had hit his brakes and as I slowed down he would speed up.

After the game, as we were waiting to get out of the parking lot, Joe spotted a gap in the line of cars. He put that stationwagon into reverse and floored it. I thought I was about to be rammed, so I put the T.Bird into reverse and floored it as well(God watches over fools and the young.) He then put the car into a skid and slid 45 degrees to make a turn into the gap. I took a more conventional route.

I consider music to be a team sport for all must blend to be in tune. Stars in a jazz band learn how to fade in and out of the spot or they will not have a spot light to shine in. Its the difference between winning and wanting to be good.

Senior year, the jazz band was scheduled to play at 3:00 p.m. at a dedication for a new health center at 23 Clover Street in Falcon Heights. Being typical kids who lived in the area for a long time, none of us asked if that was 23 North Clover or 23 South Clover.

At twenty minutes to 3:00, I set out with half the trumpet section for the health center. We turned north on Clover, to discover we should have gone south. With warp speed we headed south. At ten minutes to 3:00 we found that Clover has been turned into a one-way street for the day and we were going the wrong way. With time ticking away I had to floor it around the corner. I raced through four stop signs, came to a screeching sliding stop in front of a state trooper (who was in shock) waved to him while running for the band stand.

It was two minutes to 3:00 when I sat in my seat. The band consisted of the three trumpet players, a pianist, a drummer and the band director, and of course, my saxophone. The band director had promised to start at three on the dot. So at 3:00 he raised the baton and we began to play.

The song he selected was a familiar one. As we played, other band members arrived and took their places, found their spot and started to blow. When the time came for the sax solo, I was about to stand up when John arrived and headed straight for the solo mike. John had played this song with us a thousand and one times. and all those thousand and on times he had played the exact same solo. Perhaps because of the fact he was late, he played something that had never heard come out of his sax ever.

For about three seconds the entire band came to a halt, even the band director, amazed at what he was not playing. In those three seconds of dead air, John kept playing and the crowd was screaming. This was the first indication that something was going on.

He lost track of where we were in the music and each of us guessed where he should be. Things were a little rough behind John as each section came into line. The trumpets matched up, the trombones, the saxes. Were we in sync as a band? We kept trying to get back in tempo and time. The director is mouthing which stanza is coming up, but we are too intent to notice.

When John finishes his solo, the crowd is on its feet. We fear that things will be thrown. The sax section reaches the end of the song, unfortunately, the only ones at the end of the song. The director is still conducting, the trumpets, trombones, drums and piano are making noises. So collectively, the sax section backtracks to where they think everyone else is, just as the trumpet section ends. They then realize the mistake and jump backwards. As the trumpets backtrack, we in the sax section end, but this time we hold that last note and wait for the others to catch up. The trombones reach the end and hold their note, together we wait for the trumpets. Somehow, the tune ends, and we prepare ourselves for boos.

Instead, it was the greatest ovation we had ever received! The crowd was convinced that everything was planned. We decided not to do an encore, and left a disappointed crowd wishing for more. Believe me, we did not consider this a victory.

My cousin arrived first with her husband. Other nurses came to console her as the news spread. Her father arrived, then my father's sisters, then Jason and Honey. I never saw her so low. We had a hard time getting her to leave the bed side.

At home, I went to bed. When I awoke I discovered that the kitchen, living room and hallway were freshly painted. My mother had commented that the room needing painting. No sooner than she said it, a group of her nieces and nephews bought paint and spent the night fixing up the place to ease her mind.

My father's mail car had been sitting in front of the picture window for months, looking at it made my mother upset. It disappeared behind a tow truck within the hour. If she had said she wanted to ride on the space shuttle, I believe the assembled group of people would have made it possible.

Chapter nine

We are the world

We chose an oak casket. I turned to the funeral director.

"I hope you don't plan to give us this one. It's got scratches all over it. Do you have another one in stock?"

"Well, we could order one. It would take time though."

"I don't care."

"I'll see to it," he said.

"And make sure they waxand polish it." (I saw my mother suppress a grin. She said I sounded just like my father).

Until it was towed away, a mail car had always been in my life. Any time I needed change, all I need do was check the floor. I have memories of eight of them. The last one was in 1980 (a '79 Plymouth), the '57 Ford Fairlane was the longest lasting. That car was two-tone, brown and beige. The hood opened, not from the front, but the back. Starting in '68, Daddy bought five Plymouths in a row. All of them duds.

When he started to place the "U.S. Mail" sign on top of his cars, with flashing lights at night, and at a distance they looked like police cares. Daddy loved big cars. Plymouth made big cars and put small engines in them. The car he bought was the one advertised to get you to the lot, the car no one buys after they see what options are not included. Radios were not important to him.

Power brakes were, but not power steering (drive a big car without power steering and you do not need to lift weights.)

Once, someone stole his mail car. They caught the guy in front of a police station, with the lights on top flashing, he was a dead give away.

When he drove, it was if you were in a Rolls. Once during a blizzard, he drove this rear-wheel, six cylinder boat twelve miles to pick me up at the train station. We made it back in one piece as well, without his special snow tires. Before the state outlawed them, he owned a set of snow tires that looked like they had four inch spikes.

The last car, a Plymouth, was a rolling piece of rust in 1989, much like the '57 when we first moved. (That old Ford was the prime reason people thought he worked at the house. That car did not fit the pattern for the house and the Thunderbird. He kept it parked in front of the house to confuse people). You couldn't put anything in the trunk of that Plymouth without worrying about it falling through a hole. The passenger side door did not open. The driver side window if rolled down, would not come up again, unless you were prepared to dismantle the door frame. The tires were not a matching set. But, when my mother asked me to pick up Jeffrey at the High school, I drove the mail car.

Jeffrey wanted to hide when I pulled up. One of his friends with him didn't seem concerned. All the way home Jeffrey kept repeating, "I knew it. I just knew you were going to drive this car. I almost told Ma not to let you come pick me up. I knew it, I should have hid the keys."

"You want to get out and walk?"

"No."

"Then shut up."

As a child, Jeffrey made threats about getting out and leaving. Whenever he said those things around me I would start packing his bags.

"What are you doing."

"You said you wanted to leave. I'm helping you. Which suit do you want."

"Stop."

"You said you wanted to leave."

"I didn't mean it."

"Don't ever say things you don't mean."

As an infant, Jeffrey was light skinned and had eyes that start out blue then darken. Daddy went to visit and stood outside that room where they bring the newborns to the windows. The nurse on duty didn't check the name tags. She kept bringing dark babies to the window for Daddy to coo at.

I have an autographed baseball of Ernie Banks. The day I got it, Jeffrey demanded that I turn it over to him. I refused. He cried for the next eight hours to have that ball. My mother wanted me to give it to him, just to shut him up. Daddy offered me money. I refused them all.

I took Jeffrey and the ball to play at a near by lake. I got out a paper sack and pretended to place the ball into it. I palmed the ball and placed a rock in the sack.

"You can't always get your way in life. I would rather no one had this ball, than let you have it by way of a tantrum. I tossed the sack into the lake. For about 15 seconds, Jeffrey was uncertain. He knew me too well. He knew I wasn't about to throw that ball away. He realized that I was not going to give the ball up for any reason. He stopped asking for it.

When I look at my autographed baseball, I wonder why people mistake jerks for heros. I never thought of Peter Rose as a hero for after all, he did spike Ernie. As far as I was concerned, Rose was the last person in the world I would want to be like. Any single minded pursuit of a goal that takes place at the expense of others must be questioned.

Jackie Robinson's single minded pursuit was for a greater goal. He is the greatest all-star. He paid the price of admission for many that followed him. If money, or the game itself, is the most important thing, it can never be the stuff of a hero.

How many persons does it take to make a people? The song *We are the world* has been criticized as self-serving. Perhaps it is, but how many I's make a we? Who takes responsibility? Somewhere it must start with a me. One day recently I heard a six year old sing an anti-drug song. Much as I used to sing the Mickey Mouse song, he was singing, “Say no to drugs.”

We talk about the evils of violence, we want to ban certain things from the stores and from the boob tube. If television can trigger bad, it can trigger good. You can make fun of a movie like *Guess who's coming to dinner* and say that Sydney Poitier was too perfect. Why wouldn't he be acceptable? That is the whole point. That is the key. He had to be perfect to cause that first crack against prejudice to appear. Even the slightest defect on his part would give the hater an excuse to not consider his worth.

When I was young I resented the peace movement. I resented the use of the rhetoric in the civil rights movement. I resented it because it ignored the price one must be willing to pay. Ride a bus, you could get killed. Walk and you risk dogs and fire hoses. When the students at Kent State burned a building, when protesters threw rocks at armed troops, the first thought in my head was: What did they think? Because they were white they could ridicule, irritate and hurt with impunity?

Last of all I could not agree their treatment of returning troops. Right or wrong a man who is willing to die for his country is more an idealist than the person who protests in safety.

I did not believe the war would continue through my time in high school. My question was, “could I kill someone?” When the answer was maybe, I registered for the draft. It was my duty and obligation as a citizen of the United States of America. Unless I was 100 percent sure of the negative, I had to give America the benefit of the doubt.

The war was not a big topic in my high school. We looked at history and said: Civil War, World War I and II, Korean War... Vietnam will not last another four years. I had a greater fear of what could happen to me in this country than I did overseas.

Protest of the war, I felt, had to be along the lines of Muhammad Ali. Personal. You, the person, refuse to go. You, the person, make no comments about those who choose to fight. You, the person, give up certain things to protest what you believe. Last of all, you vote out of office those with whom you do not agree. You work toward that end.

In graduate school, I was asked to act in a video, playing a militant who takes over a TV station. The script called for me to take the American flag, spit on it and dash it to the floor. I could not do it, nor would I allow anyone else to do it. Up to the moment I had the flag in my hand I thought I could. It was only acting. Faced with the flag in my hand, only one thought came to mind. People have died to protect this flag. Coffins are draped in it. I can not spit on that faith. It does not matter if the flag is flown where it does not belong. Honor dictates that you protect it until you can get it home. My ancestors came here as slaves. We are here to stay. That is my flag. I will protect the honor of my people. Jason was a soldier at this time, I may not have liked him much, but I could not let anyone spit on his faith.

I wanted to cheer for the protesters. I could not. They did not take a higher ground. They only took an opposite side.

After I wrecked the Thunderbird, Daddy did not buy a new car until I was ready to go to the senior prom. Then he went and bought a land yacht (a black '98 Buick Regency) that had been reprocessed from a bank. The car had everything on it, everything but good gas mileage. Daddy wanted me to go to the prom in style.

People say that one of the problems is the lack of black role models. That is a lie. The problem is *access* to these role models and the responsibility of each individual to promote these people.

I discovered Duke Ellington when I was to play a solo on the saxophone. Having trouble getting the sound I wanted, I went to the hi-fi at home and looked at the albums, None of which were dated after 1963. One record was a collection of Ellington recordings from the '40s. In a song called *Just a sittin' and a rockin'*, I found my sound. I also found a hero. Whenever I had the chance I would play Ellington for my teachers. One day I came in to find the symphony conductor had borrowed my Ellington Album *New Orleans Suite*. He was using it to teach composition.

While in graduate school, Jane started researching a man named Paul Robeson. She knew I worked in downtown Chicago and asked me to pick up a bio on him. I had never heard of this man. While I was waiting for the train, a lady came up to me, looking at the book in my hand. "I used to listen to him when I was small. He had the greatest, purest and deepest tones. We all listened to him. Bought all of his records."

On the train, an old man leaned over and whispered,

"I knew him. Great man. Yes, he was. Voice like an angel."

When I went to play practice, the director noticed the book and started to sing, *Ol' Man River*, then he named six other songs that he claimed were made famous by Robeson. I had never heard of the man! These white people were telling me of this black man.

I kept the biography for a while, to read of his accomplishments and how in the 1950s there was an attempt to wipe out, in the United States of America, all knowledge of his achievements. Fear of being associated with communists has been the down fall of many a black ambition. To promote black heros is to bring into the open why many turned the wrong way.

I had to speak at my father's funeral, to say things that were more than fancy rhetoric, words to put his life in the proper content.

I went in search of the Underwood to compose my eulogy. It was in his closet, neglected and rusted, unusable. I went into the basement and searched for paper to write on. As I looked I found words I had written when Slurp died, which had appeared in the school's literary magazine. I took the magazine around and had people write there names in it. The only native American girl at my high school, and the most prettiest, wrote:

This is a beautiful story. Only someone with pure thoughts could have written it. Stay as sweet as you are.

An Act of Mercy

by William Lucas

B

"It won't hurt, will it Daddy?"

"No, Tommy, it won't hurt, it's the only thing we can do. Do you understand that?"

"Yes, yes I do." (Even though he didn't).

I

"How much longer till we get there, Daddy?"

"Not long." (Why? Why?)

(I wish I could stick my head out the window one last time, feel the wind rushing by, if only I could get up, maybe if I tried...)

"Be still, it won't be long now."

(Yes. Be still. Hope we get there soon. I don't want to throw up in the car. Not in front of Tommy).

"He's sick, Daddy, he's sick!" (Of course he's sick. Are you just now realizing that? You didn't get this way when you grandfather...)

N

"Put him on the table."

(What's that long pointed thing? No. NO!)

"He's crying Daddy, he's crying!"

"Let's go outside, son, he won't feel a thing. Stop crying now." (I might stop too.)

G

(Got to keep my eyes open...got to...so tied...if only- could rest...)

"It won't be long now."

(I remember...Tommy and I running...getting spanked...eating cigars...Christmas...waiting...sleeping...guarding the house).

O

"He's dead!"

"Mommy, Mommy, they've killed my dog!"

(Bingo was his name)

OH!

The only thing I regret about putting Slurp to sleep was that the vet didn't wait for the shot to take effect. Slurp awoke with a vengeance, he grabbed for me and tried to hold on. I can still see his eyes, as he was taken away.

Chapter ten

A raisin in the sun

I went to the post office where my father had worked for four decades to get information concerning his pension and life insurance. His records now were stored in Washington, D.C., but I would have to write to Pennsylvania for information. After receiving the Washington, D.C. info, I would send notification back to Pennsylvania who would send me forms to fill out and return for processing. As I rose to leave the clerk announced:

"I have the forms here, but I can't give them to you as it would only confuse things. You have to wait for them to send you the forms."

"You don't have a number I can call to have the forms mailed to me?"

"You can get that when you write for information."

I don't know why, but I drove into Indiana and went into the first post office I saw. I told them my father, a former postal employee had died and could I get some information about what had to be done to collect benefits for my mother.

I was taken to see the Postmaster, who gave me numbers I could call and the names of real people.

"If you have any problems, just give me a call," he said. This from a total stranger.

I mailed the request for information Federal Express. I sent the notification of death by Federal Express. I sent the two sets of forms, one for pension and one for life insurance, Federal Express. Four weeks later, we were still waiting for an acknowledgment or progress report. I wrote to President Bush about one of those points of light and the life insurance checks for Jason, my mother and Jeffrey came in. My check was lost in the mail. I did not rush to have the check stopped and a new one sent. Instead, I waited. Three weeks later my check arrived with the wrong zip code on it.

While attending school nights to obtain my Masters Degree, I took part in a production of Arthur Miller's *A view from the bridge*, the story of an Italian-American family. The father has an abnormal love for his daughter and turns illegal aliens over to immigration, rather than see his daughter fall in love with someone else. The show was well received and the cast had fun and got along like family.

The local critic came to review the show. The critic felt that a black girl portraying the daughter of an Italian, ruined the dynamics of the show as the feelings portrayed were not convincing in this context. The girl lacked the beauty and grace of feature that would make this part work.

During a production of *Five on the black hand side*, a show in which the director and cast was black and everyone else was white, a misunderstanding arose. Comments were made.

"If this were a white show the set would be ready by now."

"They are treating us like children."

"They are always late, I have not seen a rehearsal start on time. If I hear CPT again as a reason, I'll scream. (CPT-Colored People Time)

I found myself trying to explain:

"Look, this man treats everyone the same. His personality resembles a porcupine. Look how he treats his crew! Does he treat them any worse or better than you? You can call the man a jerk, not a racist."

"Hey, I've worked with you on five productions. I understand you. A white person will just call you an asshole. A black person will call you a racist. Let me just explain that you are an asshole and everything will be fine."

The same critic saw this show and loved it. I was in this show, as was the girl held accountable for her skin tone. Both shows were well received by the audience. One show was like family, one show was almost torn apart by racial tension. One show got better after the review, one show came close to not going on. Was the critic saying the black performer can not do a role justice if the part calls for white? Was the critic saying it was okay for an Irish-American to play Italian-American, but not okay for a light skinned black to play an Italian-American? There are Italians darker skinned than this girl!

I like playing comedies because in dramas I was playing too many servants and pimps. In comedy if you can get the audience to laugh you can get the part. And if my character takes off on Boris Karloff, John Wayne, Al Jolsen or Jackie Gleason, it is even funnier.

In high school, I competed in original comedy monologues, after I had convinced the sponsors that what I wanted to say was funny. At first, I had a hard time doing this. In an effort to get me to see the correct point of view, I was taken to a competition and told to watch other performers and see what they did. I reported that they were stealing material from Bill Cosby, Richard Pryor and Jonathan Winters, to name a few. I had not seen anything original. I was too dense to take a hint, so, the next competition, I was allowed to compete. With my bits of warped wisdom, I walked away with more points than the other 9 people from Boone High combined. After that, I was left on my own.

At first, I was told that I had weak material, but good delivery. By the end of the season, I was told good material, but poor delivery. I was good enough for my fellow competitors to try to un-nerve me. They would tape my efforts, then make faces and try not to laugh when I performed.

Things might have been different if not for the judge of my first competition. I stayed for some unofficial criticism. He told me I dressed wrong, I wasn't funny, my material lacked substance. He did not have a single positive statement to make. I was now willing to listen to what anyone at Daniel Boone had to say and was almost not going into the next competition, when my sponsor came up and said, "I heard you were great."

"What do you mean?"

"I was just talking to your judge." My judge, after telling me negative things, told the first adult he met (my sponsor) of the funniest comic he had seen in four years of judging such events. The judge was not aware he was talking to my sponsor; and although the name of this fantastic black comic was not given, the jokes retold were mine.

I always used bad jokes to lead off.

> "Do you know why the Volkswagen was crying?"
>
> "Someone ran over his pet Beetle."
>
> "Hear about the Volkswagen entered in the Indianapolis 500?"
>
> "Made a pit stop and fell in."
>
> "Do you know what's in back of a jet powered Volkswagen?"
>
> "Can of Raid, going full blast?"
>
> "I know you're thinking these aren't funny. And if you would stop laughing, I would tell better ones. There you go again. Okay, this one's really bad. How long has corn been around?"
>
> "About as long as I've been telling these jokes. There you go again."
>
> "It's the trees... The trees! They're planning to take over the world. Its because of Big Red! You've all heard of Big Red haven't you? He was the biggest, most widely respected red wood tree in the entire ed wood forest. That is, until he was cut down and turned into toilet paper. Well, the other trees didn't like this. They were tired of people cutting them down and turning them into furniture. They were tired of people scratching "I Love You" in their bark. I ask you, how would you like someone to

carve words on you as a sign of sentiment. For someone you don't even know! And dogs! They were sick of all those dogs that couldn't find fire hydrants.

Well, the trees went out and elected a President. President Woodrow Willow. You've heard of Woodrow Willow haven't you? Well, Willow decided to train the leaves. The leaves would change colors when ever people thought bad things about them. Well, sometime that October, all the leaves started to change colors. It was a sign, the people were up to no good.

Willow decided it was time to teach the world not to mess with trees. The trees control the wind you know. Yeah! Think of all the destruction caused by whirlwinds, hurricanes and tornadoes. Don't you realize that they are caused by the trees shaking all those leaves up, stirring up all that wind? Yeah!

I can tell by the way you're looking at me that you find this a little bit odd. But wait...on the way home yesterday...I saw my son raking leaves. He had made a pile of leaves. As he turned his back I saw the leaf pile inching toward him. Then they leaped on him. And right before my eyes he was transformed into a maple tree. All up and down the street I saw other people transformed into all kinds of wood. It got so bad, I couldn't see the forest, all the trees were in the way.

I think that the trees felt that if everyone was a tree, no one would cut them down. I ran into the house to tell my wife about our son. I found her in the bedroom, growing out of the bed, a white birch. And growing next to her, limbs intertwined a Douglas fir.

I don't have much time. On the way over a leaf touched me. I think I'm turning into a Walnut. You have to go out and tell the world, that the only hope for mankind is to turn over a new leaf.

Speaking of turning over a new leaf... An odd thing happened about this time last Christmas. My door bell rang, no that's not the odd part. I went to the door, there was a white man at it. You don't find many white people in my neighborhood, not at night anyway. And this guy, he wore a red suit. He had a white beard. I know what you are thinking. But this dude was skinny. six foot, hundred pound skinny. And he said,

"Excuse me, I've got a couple of injured deer out here. I could use some help."

I almost shut the door right then, but I was curious. He didn't seem drunk.

"I guess the elves were right," he said. "They told me no one believes any more. The elves are realists. They don't want to make toys, they want to leave the North Pole, move into a treehouse and make cookies. There's always a market for cookies they say. That's what I used to say about toys."

"If you're Santa," I said. "Why are you so skinny?"

"The elves have been on strike. They want more work. And the reindeer just don't fly as high as they used to. And me, well...I kept thinking of the good old days before radar. I started to lose weight, over two hundred pounds. My health became poor, I was in constant pain. You can not imagine the agony I went through just by going Ho, Ho, Ho. I went to a doctor. he tried to have me committed.

I think the wind blew us off course. I'm just not sure. I remember hearing a shot, then a scream, my scream, "Pull up! Pull up!" But we crashed...into a rice patty. Some soldiers came along and helped me bail out the sleigh. I left them some G.I Joe's, and we took off. It was awhile before I noticed the blood. We started for home, but had to land here.

If you will help me get Donner into the sleigh, I think we can make it back"

I knew I had him then. I would follow him outside and there would be Candid Camera. Something. There was something out there. Eight standing deer, one on the ground. For a deer he was real light. Flying deer, I guess, have to be. Hollow bones, I think.

I watched them take off. I don't believe it either.
That's what you get when you stop laughing.
I thank you for your time.

*****

One person can make the difference. That person can be a stranger, anyone willing to step in and say this is wrong. When that one responsible person points the finger at the Emperor, all can see that he is naked and always was.

The tide changed at Cherokee the day Elise pointed. Our teacher had asked everyone in the class to describe what kind of American they were. I was the only one to say simply American.

"Why is that William. Aren't you a Black American?"

"I just want to be known as an American."

"Aren't you proud to be a Black American? Or an African-American?"

At which point Elise stood up and said, "I think William is right. I want to be just an American too."

Half the girls in the class changed from being irish, Polish, German, etc. to simple Americans. None of the boys changed.

I was losing contact with my old Cherokee Springs friends. I never forgot those who had stood up for me in my time of need. Duke Ellington was in town, so I convinced my father to take a group of us to see him. I asked about 10 people. Sam had other commitments, Joe didn't like the Duke. About six said yes. The last person I asked was Elise, and she became excited saying that Ellington was one of her favorites.

One by one they all canceled. Elise called.

"Sorry William. My parents will not let me go. They don't think it would be safe."

Daddy offered to take me anyway. I said no.

*****

As we prepared for the funeral, in that days mail we received our first letter threatening to sue us for nonpayment of medical bills. My father belonged to a HMO. I discovered that after 65, HMO's consider themselves the secondary carrier to Medicare. Medicare is a slow pay. HMO is a pre-pay plan. There should have been no bills to pay, let alone law suits. The letter came from an attorney in California representing a self-incorporated doctor in Illinois. The trick of the trade is to send a bill to the patient and if they pay terrific. If the patient questions the bill, it's all a mistake.

By the end of the month my mother received eight different medical bills. She called each office. Each office said it was an error. A week would go by and a new bill would appear from the office. Anyone of those bills would have wiped out my mothers savings.

I discovered that as far as pensions are concerned, they serve best those who only think of themselves. Without a survivor benefit, my father would have received 80 percent of his salary at retirement. With a survivor benefit this was reduced to 70. After Daddy's death this was lowered to 60 percent.

His life insurance policy was a winner as well. Each pay period for 42 years he paid toward a life insurance policy. At his retirement he was faced, because of his health, with premiums of $200 a month. He declined them, so his policy reduced itself 2% a month after his 65th birthday. The sum he believed he was leaving behind was reduced by 44% at his death (max reduction was 75%). People will talk all day about why whole life policies are a waste of time. They are lured into cheap term policies worth larger amounts, if you die while you are still a good risk.

Whenever I am asked if I want extra term life insurance, I say no.

"Why," they always ask.

"Because you are betting I don't die. After 70 you don't cover me at all. So I pay in for the next 40 years and have nothing but peace of mind. Well, I don't plan to die either. Regular coverage is fine with me."

I remember a time, the subscription department of a newspaper had called to find out why Daddy had canceled his service.

"Because I reported a dead body and you didn't send anyone out."

The lady on the other end hung up.

When Jeffrey got his first saxophone, the rental service called Daddy to question some of the replies he had put on his credit application.

"Mr. Lucas, you wrote down that you have been employed at the same establishment for 34 years, is that correct."

"Yes, it is."

"You have a son ten?"

"Yes."

"Would you be willing to furnish proof?"

"Are you calling me a liar?"

"It is a bit odd. Most of the parents are 34, not employed 34 years."

"Where did you learn to read. You have my age. You have my employer. You have the name of my bank. What you don't have is me as a customer."

Daddy hung up.

Chapter eleven

The shepard who watches over the night flock

At the final performance of *Five on the black hand side*, the Chicagoland area suffered severe flooding and heavy fog. I left the house at 6:00 p.m. for a 6:30 call and arrived at 7:15, one of the first people at the theater. The show was to go on at 8:00. At 8:15 we had only part of a cast and not a single person in the audience. Our director said we would wait.

9:45p.m., still missing two members of the cast, we opened the show. The house was full, standing room only. People were begging to be allowed to stand by the door and watch. Fire laws prevented it.

We hear that black shows are not a draw. We are told repeatedly that blacks will not support the arts. That night, I believed a line from the show instead.

"Piss on my back and tell me its raining."

I called the Roy Leonard Show, WGN radio and asked where the Duke Ellington Orchestra was playing. He gave me tickets. Jane and I went to this night club type establishment in the south Suburbs that had its nightly revue. That night they were presenting us with a shortened version of the two hour program.

Twenty minutes into the revue I saw the band bus arrive. Forty-five minutes into the revue I saw the band members standing at the wings. Fifty minutes into the revue I thought that if this is the shortened version I did not want the long one.

Ninety minutes after they were to perform, Mercer Ellington led his men to the stage which was about one foot too small. One member of each section had to place his chair on the floor. Mercer wished us welcome and introduced the first number. During a long solo in which the tenor saxophone player strolled among the patrons, a bus driver walked in and announced it was time to go. As sixty senior citizens go up to leave, the player continued to perform.

The hour grew late and finally Mercer turned to we few who remained.

"For our loyal fans, we are going to keep playing until you ask us to stop."

The band was listed for two shows. Ellington announced a third. Our waitress, now off work, asked if she could sit at our table. We didn't mind. They really got down then. At 2:00a.m., Mercer said the band needed a break. They, he said, would continue.

The music of Duke Ellington changed the course of my life. He did more than make pleasing sounds. Solos were more than technique. When I read what Duke had to say about Bubber Miley, I had the key.

"...Every note he played was soul filled with the pulse of compulsion. Before they played his choruses he would tell his story, and he always had a story for his music, such as: 'This is an old man, tired from working in the field's since sunup, coming up the road in the sunset or on his way home for dinner. He's tired but strong, and humming in time with his broken gait.'"

Edward Kennedy Ellington: *Music is My Mistress* (New York: Double day & Co., 1973) Page 106.

Telling stories, painting pictures in music. Each title a clue, each song a story. Portraits with notes. The album I found that day was entitled: *In a Mellow Tone. Just A-Settin' and A-Rockin'* featuring the tenor sax of Ben Webster, the unique sound of "Tricky Sam" Naton's trombone. The more I read about the man the more intrigued I became. He traveled through the south on his own private train. This way, there were no hassles about where he stayed.

> "In order to avoid problems, we used two Pullman sleeping cars and a seventy-foot baggage car. Everywhere we went in the South, we lived in them... Many observers would say, 'Why that's the way the President travels!' It automatically gained us respect from the natives, and removed the threat and anticipation of trouble...." Edward Kennedy Ellington: *Music is My Mistress* (New York: Doubleday & Co., 1973) Page 86, 87.

Ellington formed his first band in 1918 of four people. Sonny Greet, drummer, the last member of this original group left Ellington's organization in 1951. Between 1918 and 1974, when Duke died, nine musicians had stayed a decade, seven for twenty years, three for over thirty, and one, Harry Carney, Baritone Saxophone, for forty-eight years. They say many in the group would not talk to one another.

When I found the album entitled *70th Birthday Concert*, I found my theme. One song, one recording, the song, *Black Butterfly*, the soloist; Johnny Hodges, alto sax. When I heard Duke say that dissonance is our way of life and that blacks are something apart, yet an integral part of American society, I thought of this song.

Ellington begins with a series of scales that set the scene, followed by the weaving texture of woody toned clarinets (Like a field of flowers). Then as Duke shouts "Go." Enter the Butterfly. With a swooping-sad sound in discord with the underlying beauty...the sax lays down cords of rich resonance. He is both a part and at a distance. The two are separate but equal. One can not exist without the other. The beauty is the contrast.

With soaring swings of grace, with matchless tone and speech-like cadences, we hear and see the butterfly. We feel its joy in floating. We sense its struggle to stay aloft amidst changing currents. The beauty is the flight, not in where its been or where it will go.

Then as he flutters out of sight, we marvel at what has been. And wait for his return.

Someone once asked what was the greatest big band?

"I think you really have to say two. Basie for what a big band does best. Ellington for what a big band can do."

I saw Cootie Williams play, which may not seem much to most people. In a world of instant fame and amplified noise few remember side men. He trumpeted for the Duke;left Ellington (a song was written about it) to play with Benny Goodman. Cootie left Goodman to form his own band. The song *Round Midnight* lists Cootie as one of the composers, was the theme song of his group. Then after twenty years or so, Cootie returned to Duke's band.

He was famous for the use of the plunger and the growl. He had a sound that was big and fat. One did not have to be told who was playing when he was on stage, you knew. He was Bubber Miley's replacement. He is in the jazz hall of fame.

Mercer was leading the band. It was an out door free concert at night in a shopping center parking lot. Someone kept shouting for *Take the A Train*, but when Mercer looked his way, Cootie shook his head no. The Duke was dead, Cootie would have his way. The A Train would be delayed.

Mr. Williams looked like a man who had been on the wrong side of one too many fights. He looked old and mean. I wondered if it was all a mistake. He looked like he should be in a retirement home not heading for a solo mike. They were going to play *The Shepard Who Watches Over the Night Flock*, a song that is on *The Second Sacred Music Concert* Album. This was a song I had played many times but I never heard the band when Duke was alive. All the famous people were gone. Nothing was like what I had thought. The piano was just an instrument and not the center.

Then Cootie put the horn to his lips. I knew then what I had read was all true. What I had head on record was real. On a recording made in concert a decade before, Cootie had missed his intro. The crowd laughs while Duke vamps until Mr. Williams is ready. Before he begins he speaks:

"Old man now, man... Can't play all those fast numbers. Out of air."

Then he plays *Echos of Harlem* and the echoes are of both the past and the musician he once was. His tone is fractured, sound full of air. Still the majestic lion, still able to make you listen and not care about the flaws.

Here he was in person. He played slowly and deliberately, and like a dinosaur out of time, played with a power and soul that transcended time, age and ill health. Not many people can make time stand still. You heard the mistakes, the inability to hit certain notes and did not care. I did not care. I was not alone. He had a mike in front of him, but the mike was not a crutch to help his sound reach out to the crowd, something that would save his strength. The mike was perhaps, even in the way. Few held the light the way he did. When he paused for breath, I thought it would be his last. He was just warming up. As he took out the mute, the crowd roared its approval. He started to play open horn, when he ended and was putting the mute back in, he obtained a standing ovation. Growling, and playing like there would be no tomorrow, he played. I wanted it to end and I wanted it to go on forever. This was a kind of stage presence, you only think you know exists in the world. The song ended, and Cootie received a second standing ovation. As he bowed, Mercer started into *Take the A Train*, Cootie was stuck so he played.

Afterward, someone approached Cootie for an autograph. "I'll hold your horn, just sign the album."

Mr. Williams looked at the man, "No one touches my horn man." and he walked away. For me, hearing him play was more than enough.

Don't know who Cootie Williams is? Well, I went to a Jazz camp and one of the instructors asked that same question. When I raised my hand, it was not what he expected. The instructor feeling his point was lost, said to me, "He doesn't know who you are either."

I thought the instructor was mean. Moments of magic are rare. I heard the man play.

The world is full of heros that don't make the news. People who make magic. Ella Fitzgerald did. I felt her before I saw her on the stage. The whole stage lit up. She sang to the entire crowd. She made you believe you alone had her eye.

Count Basie, I saw three times. The first time when he played something unexpected on the piano, he looked to see if anyone noticed. He saw me, and winked.

The second time I saw Basie was right after Duke Ellington had died. Basie went to the mike and said, "I would like to play this next one for a friend now gone." He played *Take the A Train.*

The third time, someone in the crowd shouted, "You're the greatest." To which the Count replied, "Yes, I know."

Richard Burton was touring in *Camelot*, during the curtain call he made this little speech,

"I know many of you are here tonight to see me, but there are two bus loads of people from a small town in Iowa here to see someone else." He walked into the chorus line and brought forth a girl (someone I did not even notice in the show) and gave her family a chance to see her close up.

Before a Chicago Jazz Festival appearance, Ray Charles rehearsed for two hours. He had an audience of early comers who saw a better show than the one he gave that night. He played songs that weren't polished enough for the night, songs that were all the more special for it. Being early, no one cared how close you came to the stage. You could even talk to Ray. The Chicago Jazz Festival is full of special sights and sounds. One year, a giant poster of Duke Ellington was on stage. Harold Ashby and his trio were performing a lackluster set, when suddenly the wind blew and the poster shook. Harold looked over his shoulder and announced, "Just Squeeze Me." He started to play with a new power and rhythm, He evoking memories of hugs and tender smiles. Someone started dancing in the aisles, then more and more. Later, Harold said he felt the Duke looking over his shoulder.

I remember Lionel Hampton playing during a thunderstorm with lightening flashing in the background. A bass player who had earlier bragged about how he was going to play with Hampton. As Hampton played, this player who appeared to be high on something, said Lionel had kicked him off the stage.

"But, he's cool man. He's right. I wasn't ready."

I have walked away from many a jazz concert with memories frozen in time. Roy Eldridge, doing *Drop me off up town* and singing the Anita O'Day parts.

A teacher at college once told everyone to bring their favorite records and the class would listen to them. I brought the Ray Charles recording of *America the Beautiful.* Afterward the teacher said to me,

"Why are you trying to impose your propaganda on the class. That's not your favorite song."

It was, it is.

It does not matter what others say. I heard Cootie Williams play. I learned from the Duke about the most important of freedoms when I read *Music is My Mistress* by Edward Kennedy Ellington. "...freedom from hate, unconditionally; freedom from self-pity (even throughout all the pain and bad news); freedom from fear of possibly doing something that might help another more than it might himself; and freedom from the kind of pride that could make a man feel that he was better than his brother or neighbor." (New York: Doubleday & co.), 1973 Page 159-160.

As I composed the words to say for my father, I listened to the music of Duke Ellington. *Soul Soothing Beach, Big Fat Alice's Blues, Star Crossed Lovers, A Tone Parallel to Harlem, I'm in Another World, Prelude to a Kiss, Swamp Go, In a Sentimental Mood* and *Hit me with a Hot Note and Watch me Bounce.*

Chapter twelve

In a sentimental mood

Every summer we drove down U.S. highway 41 to Kentucky. The best of the drive was three miles of curves known as Turkey Run. It was part of the glory of visiting my mother's parents. They had an outhouse and a water pump in the front yard.

Kentucky was different than Illinois. The people talked funny, and the dirt was red. Sometimes when it rained, one side of the street would stay dry. That never happened in Illinois.

Kentucky had miles of gravel roads with trees that looked like they had silk hanging from them. And buckeyes. And of course there was Luke, Grandpa's collie. Luke loved to race cars. Once you pulled into the gravel road leading to my grandparents farm, Luke would appear and start to run in the fields along side the road, appearing and disappearing among the trees. When we reached the one lane bridge just before the house, Luke would go down the ravine and into the creek and up the side. Luke would be a leaping muddy mess waiting for us to pull into the driveway. It was part of what made the visit so special.

Granny kept her granchildren's favorite ice cream in a freezer. There would be a barbecue, and of course, there was a 1947 mint condition Chrysler, so dark a purple that at a distance it looked black. The knobs on the radio were made of ivory. The seats had the material you would find on a living room couch. All my aunts and uncles would fight over who would drive this car. It didn't matter what car you arrived in, or how new or fast it was, that Chrysler was the car of choice for any trip that had to be made. Grandchildren fought over the right to wash it.

We would scrub that car so hard that the paint would come off. We even washed the spare tire. It was one of those big cars with running boards, a single windshield washer (that came down from the top) and a hood ornament of an eagle. It was in a garage so decrepit that if one breathed too hard the walls would shake.

This was a tobacco farm. Every morning Grandpa would walk the fields, and in the evening Grandpa would feed the hogs. I went with him once. He would snip the heads off tobacco worms without a thought. And he would take us fishing.

The house had a pot belly wood stove in the living room. The house had all the modern conveniences, but they were treated as luxury items. Even the water that came from the faucet was considered a luxury. Out front was a tree with a wood swing. And all around the house were the flowers my grandmother had planted.

After the house caught fire and burned down, the Chrysler was sold and Granny and Grandpa moved north. The family reunions ceased to be special. No more big freezer full of ice cream. No Luke (who refused to leave the farm and always ran back to it) and no big old car.

With Granny and Grandpa up north, I no longer visited Aunt May and Uncle Billy who lived in an old mansion, that was built overlooking the river, until the river changed course and left the house overlooking dirt. They lived on the first two floors and had the rest of the house closed off. Chickens were everywhere. The house was full of clocks that had pendulums and had to be wound. Each clock kept its own time. I thought of the house as a museum. I would sit in a rocking chair and watch a clock. One day Aunt May saw me looking at a light blue ashtray made of hand blown glass and covered with what I called pimples. Aunt May gave it to me.

That ashtray was my prized possession. When Aunt May died, it became an important object to my mother for it was the only thing she had that belonged to Aunt May. On the day I moved from my parents home into my own apartment, I left the ashtray behind for my mother to keep. When I began to unpack, I found that my mother had packed the ashtray without telling me. I held the ashtray and cried.

I never knew my father's parents. I have memory, but nothing I can trust. My mother still uses Mr. when referring to my father's father, who went by his initials. It was very important in those days for a black man to obtain what little respect he could from the white man. Initials prevent the whites from shortening his given name, and since one could never expect to be called Mr., being called RL was neutral that one could live with. Better than having a ten year old white boy call a sixty year old black man Bobby. RL had more dignity. One had to carve out small victories wherever one could.

Between two sets of grandparents there were fourteen children. Fourteen family units with only two divorces in the lot. I looked at the people who had come to pay their respects. According to news reports one out of every four black males between the ages of 20 and 29 is either in jail or on probation. People who cared about my father were abnormal. There should have been at least 15 probationers in the lot. Not a one.

I bought a cross to help me concentrate. I held it tightly as I walked to the podium.

"In life," I said, "One has many choices. Sometimes you have no choice at all. (Someone shouted 'That's right.') None of us chooses our parents. I and my brothers were blessed by God. ('Tell it,' someone said). God gave us parents it was so easy to be proud of! (My mother said my name at this point and I almost broke).

"In life, you can not choose your relatives. ('Yes Lord,' a voice exclaimed). And yet, all my life I have been surrounded by relatives who could make anyones' top ten list of great people to know.

"In life ('Tell it') you can choose one's friends. My father chose his friends well ('Yes, he did'). They are friends of thoughtful action and constant support. Friends ('Yes!') of caring and lasting value.

"My father chose a wife whose special value can only be compared to that of a rainbow. 'Amen').

"My father had a special eyesight. He was able to follow a path that appeared to be nothing more than an endless series of rocks and obstructions. He saw a prize worth taking a tougher road ('Yes, he did.'). He saw hope of a better world. ('Amen').

"They say we have the right to life, liberty and the pursuit of happiness ('That's what they say'). A proclamation gave us liberty ('That it did. Amen. Tell it.') For some the pursuit of happiness was second to the pursuit for equality.

"Personal dreams were often deferred. ('Yes, Lord'). Dreams had to wait for the day you would be judged for the content of your character. ('Yes, Lord'). Dreams had to wait for the day, ('Amen') you would not be judged by the color of your skin. For some that day never dame. ('So true, so true').

"For 41 years my father worked at the post office. Through rain, through sleet, through dark of night. For the people who needed their mail. ('That's right').

"Politics of the postal system wore him down ('Yes, it did Lord'). The people on his route...well...they brought him joy. ('Thank you Jesus').

"In another time, in another place, in another world, in a different America ('Tell it'), there might have been an option for what he wanted to be. Not what he was allowed to be.

"he could deliver the mail. And that job allowed him to provide an opportunity for his sons to look to the stars for dreams.

"That job allowed us to break the cycle of self-limitation. To never think of color as a second-class ticket to life. His family went first-class. ('Yes. Yes. Yes').

"Disabled veteran. He would not have gone to war for this country if he felt that equality was impossible, that freedom was an illusion. ('Amen').

"He believed in God. He accepted Christ. He expected those who set themselves up as role models, to be role models. In this, he was a hard man.

"His final years were full of pain. He suffered a great deal. He lived long enough to see grandchildren, to finish his house to know how much and how deeply he was loved.

"God gave him an Indian Summer.

"To understand my father is to understand why the caged bird sings."

I then read the poem by Maya Angelou:

A free bird leaps
on the back of the wind
and floats downstream
till the current ends
and dips his wing
in the orange sun rays
and dares to claim the sky.

But a bird that stalks
down his narrow cage
can seldom see through
his bar of rage
his wings are clipped and
his feet are tied
so he opens his throat to sing.

the caged bird sings
with a fearful trill
of things unknown
but longed for still
and his tune is heard
on the distant hill
for the caged bird
sings of freedom.

The free bird thinks of another breeze
and the trade winds soft through the sighing trees
and the fat worms waiting on a dawn-bright lawn
and he names the sky his own.

but a caged bird stands on the grave of dreams
his shadow shouts on a nightmare scream
his wings are clipped and his feet are tied
so he opens his throat to sing.

The caged bird sings
with fearful trill
of things unknown
but longed for still
and his tune is heard
on the distant hill
for the caged bird
sings for freedom.

As I left the podium, Jason rushed up to me and shook my hand. The saddest day of my life became one of my happiest.

Making lemonade

In the long history of the world, only a few generations have been granted the role of defending freedom in its hour of maximum danger. I do not believe that any of us would exchange places with any other people or any other generation. The energy, the faith, the devotion which we bring to this endeavor will light our country and all who serve it, and the glow from that fire can truly light the world.

John F. Kennedy Inaugural Address

In the process of gaining our rightful place, we must not be guilty of wrongful deeds. Let us not seek to satisfy our thirst for freedom by drinking from the cup of bitterness and hatred. We must forever conduct our struggle on the high plane of dignity and discipline.

Martin Luther King, Jr.
Washington, D.C. 1963

Dreams make life worthwhile. They give us hope when all around is hate. Dreams give us glimpses of summer. If we dream, then the visions of others will never fall into a nightmare called reality.

Gerald Thompson